Digital Techniques 3 Checkbook

J O Bird
BSc(Hons), AFIMA, TEng(CEI), MIElecIE

R E Vears

Butterworths
London Boston
Durban Singapore Sydney Toronto Wellington

All rights reserved. No part of this publication may be reproduced or
transmitted in any form or by any means, including photocopying and
recording without the written permission of the copyright holder,
application for which should be addressed to the publishers. Such written
permission must also be obtained before any part of this publication is
stored in a retrieval system of any nature.

This book is sold subject to the Standard Conditions of Sale of Net Books
and may not be resold in the UK below the net price given by the Publishers
in their current price list.

First published 1983

© Butterworth & Co (Publishers) Ltd 1983

British Library Cataloguing in Publication Data

Bird, J O, and
Vears, R E
  Digital techniques 3 checkbook.—Butterworths
technical and scientific checkbooks)
  1. Digital electronics   2. Logic, Symbolic
    and mathematical
I. Title II. Vears, R E
621.3815'3   TK7868.D5

ISBN 0-408-01801-1

Typeset by Tunbridge Wells Typesetting Services Ltd
Printed in Scotland by Thomson Litho Ltd., East Kilbride

Contents

Preface v

1 Simplification of Boolean expressions using Karnaugh maps 1
Main points 1
Worked problems 6
Further problems 12

2 Logic circuits 14
Main points 14
Worked problems 18
Further problems 33

3 Logic families 39
Main points 39
Worked problems 43
Further problems 70

4 Bistables 73
Main points 73
Worked problems 75
Further problems 93

5 Counters 95
Main points 95
Worked problems 107
Further problems 123

6 Registers 125
Main points 125
Worked problems 125
Further problems 138

7 Digital storage devices 140
Main points 140
Worked problems 142
Further problems 164

Index 167

Note to Reader

As textbooks become more expensive, authors are often asked to reduce the number of worked and unworked problems, examples and case studies. This may reduce costs, but it can be at the expense of practical work which gives point to the theory.

Checkbooks if anything lean the other way. They let problem-solving establish and exemplify the theory contained in technician syllabuses. The Checkbook reader can gain *real* understanding through seeing problems solved and through solving problems himself.

Checkbooks do not supplant fuller textbooks, but rather supplement them with an alternative emphasis and an ample provision of worked and unworked problems. The brief outline of essential data—definitions, formulae, laws, regulations, codes of practice, standards, conventions, procedures, etc—will be a useful introduction to a course and a valuable aid to revision. Short-answer and multi-choice problems are a valuable feature of many Checkbooks, together with conventional problems and answers.

Checkbook authors are carefully selected. Most are experienced and successful technical writers; all are experts in their own subjects; but a more important qualification still is their ability to demonstrate and teach the solution of problems in their particular branch of technology, mathematics or science.

Authors, General Editors and Publishers are partners in this major low-priced series whose essence is captured by the Checkbook symbol of a question or problem 'checked' by a tick for correct solution.

Preface

This textbook of worked problems provides coverage of the Technician Education Councils level 3 units in Digital Techniques (syllabuses U81/751 and U81/752). However it can also be regarded as a basic textbook in digital techniques for a much wider range of courses.

The aim of the book is to develop an understanding of the following topics related to digital electronics: Karnaugh maps, universal NAND and NOR logic, logic families, bistables, counters, registers and storage media. Each topic considered in the text is presented in a way that assumes in the reader only the knowledge attained at TEC level 2 in Digital Techniques (U81/750).
Digital Techniques 3 Checkbook provides a follow-up to the checkbook written for *Digital Techniques 2*. It contains over 160 illustrations, over 100 detailed worked problems, followed by over 150 further problems with answers.

The authors would like to express their appreciation for the friendly cooperation and helpful advice given to them by the publishers. Thanks are also due to Mrs. Elaine Woolley for the excellent typing of the manuscript. Finally, the authors would like to add a special word of thanks to their wives, Elizabeth and Rosemary, for their patience, help and encouragement during the preparation of this book.

J O Bird
R E Vears
Highbury College of Technology
Portsmouth

Butterworths Technical and Scientific Checkbooks

General Editors for Science, Engineering and Mathematics titles:
J O Bird and A J C May, Highbury College of Technology, Portsmouth.

General Editor for Building, Civil Engineering, Surveying and Architectural titles:
Colin R Bassett, lately of Guildford County College of Technology.

A comprehensive range of Checkbooks will be available to cover the major syllabus areas of the TEC, SCOTEC and similar examining authorities. A comprehensive list is given below and classified according to levels.

Level 1 (Red covers)
Mathematics
Physical Science
Physics
Construction Drawing
Construction Technology
Microelectronic Systems
Engineering Drawing
Workshop Processes & Materials

Level 2 (Blue covers)
Mathematics
Chemistry
Physics
Building Science and Materials
Construction Technology
Electrical & Electronic Applications
Electrical & Electronic Principles
Electronics
Microelectronic Systems
Engineering Drawing
Engineering Science
Manufacturing Technology
Digital Techniques
Motor Vehicle Science

Level 3 (Yellow covers)
Mathematics
Chemistry
Building Measurement
Construction Technology
Environmental Science
Electrical Principles
Electronics
Microelectronic Systems
Electrical Science
Mechanical Science
Engineering Mathematics & Science
Engineering Science
Engineering Design
Manufacturing Technology
Motor Vehicle Science
Light Current Applications

Level 4 (Green covers)
Mathematics
Building Law
Building Services & Equipment
Construction Technology
Construction Site Studies
Concrete Technology
Economics for the Construction Industry
Geotechnics
Engineering Instrumentation & Control

Level 5
Building Services & Equipment
Construction Technology
Manufacturing Technology

1 Simplification of Boolean expressions using Karnaugh maps

A MAIN POINTS CONCERNED WITH THE SIMPLIFICATION OF BOOLEAN EXPRESSIONS USING KARNAUGH MAPS

1 A Boolean expression may be used to describe a complex switching circuit or a logic system (as shown in chapters 4 and 5 of *Digital Techniques 2 Checkbook*). If the Boolean expression can be simplified, then the number of switches or logic elements can be reduced with a resulting saving in cost. Using the laws and rules of Boolean algebra, which are summarised in *Table 1* provides one method of simplification; another method is by using **Karnaugh maps,** where the function to be simplified is displayed diagrammatically on a map consisting of a grid of squares.

Table 1 Some laws and rules of Boolean algebra

Reference	Name	Rule or law
1	Commutative	$A + B = B + A$
2	laws	$A.B = B.A$
3	Associative	$(A + B) + C = A + (B + C)$
4	laws	$(A.B).C = A.(B.C)$
5	Distributive	$A.(B + C) = A.B + A.C$
6	laws	$A + (B.C) = (A + B).(A + C)$
7	Sum rules	$A + O = A$
8		$A + 1 = 1$
9		$A + A = A$
10		$A + \overline{A} = 1$
11	Product	$A.O = O$
12	rules	$A.1 = A$
13		$A.A = A$
14		$A.\overline{A} = 0$
15	Absorption	$A + A.B = A$
16	rules	$A.(A + B) = A$
17		$A + \overline{A}.B = A + B$
18	Double 'not' rule	$\overline{\overline{A}} = A$

ariable Karnaugh maps

A truth-table for a two-variable expression is shown in *Table 2(a)*, the "1" in the third row output showing that $Z = A.\bar{B}$. Each of the four possible Boolean expressions associated with a two-variable function can be depicted as shown in *Table 2(b)* in which one cell is allocated to each row of the truth table. A matrix similar to that shown in *Table 2(b)* can be used to depict $Z = A.\bar{B}$, by putting a 1 in the cell corresponding to $A.\bar{B}$ and 0's in the remaining cells. This method of depicting a Boolean expression is called a **two-variable Karnaugh map,** and is shown in *Table 2(c)*.

Table 2

| Inputs | | Output | Boolean |
A	B	Z	expression
0	0	0	$\bar{A}.\bar{B}$
0	1	0	$\bar{A}.B$
1	0	1	$A.\bar{B}$
1	1	0	$A.B$

(a)

A\B	0 (Ā)	1 (A)
0 (B̄)	$\bar{A}.\bar{B}$	$A.\bar{B}$
1 (B)	$\bar{A}.B$	$A.B$

(b)

A\B	0	1
0	0	1
1	0	0

(c)

(ii) To simplify a two-variable Boolean expression, the Boolean expression is depicted on a Karnaugh map, as outlined above. Any cells on the map having either a common vertical side or a common horizontal side are grouped together to form a **couple.** (This is a coupling together of cells, not just combining two together.) The simplified Boolean expression for a couple is given by those variables common to all cells in the couple.

(iii) The Karnaugh map shown in *Table 3* represents the Boolean expression:

$$A.\bar{B} + A.B$$

The two cells containing 1's have a common horizontal edge and thus a vertical couple, shown by the broken lines, is formed. The only variable common to both cells in the couple is $A = 1$, i.e., A. Thus

Table 3

A\B	0	1
0	0	1
1	0	1

$A.\overline{B} + A.B. = A$ (which may be checked using the laws and rules of Boolean algebra).

3 **Three-variable Karnaugh maps**
 (i) A truth table for a three-variable expression is shown in *Table 4(a)*, the 1's in the output column showing that:

$$Z = \overline{A}.\overline{B}.C + \overline{A}.B.C + A.B.\overline{C}$$

Each of the eight possible Boolean expressions associated with a three-variable function can be depicted as shown in *Table 4(b)*, in which one cell is allocated to each row of the truth table. A matrix similar to that shown in *Table 4(b)* can be used to depict: $Z = \overline{A}.\overline{B}.C + \overline{A}.B.C + A.B.\overline{C}$, by putting 1's in the cells corresponding to the Boolean terms on the right of the Boolean equation and 0's in the remaining cells. This method of depicting a three-variable Boolean expression is called a three-variable Karnaugh map, and is shown in *Table 4(c)*.

Table 4

| Inputs | | | Output | Boolean |
A	B	C	Z	expression
0	0	0	0	$\overline{A}.\overline{B}.\overline{C}$
0	0	1	1	$\overline{A}.\overline{B}.C$
0	1	0	0	$\overline{A}.B.\overline{C}$
0	1	1	1	$\overline{A}.B.C$
1	0	0	0	$A.\overline{B}.\overline{C}$
1	0	1	0	$A.\overline{B}.C$
1	1	0	1	$A.B.\overline{C}$
1	1	1	0	$A.B.C$

(a)

C \ A.B	00 ($\overline{A}\ \overline{B}$)	01 ($\overline{A}.B$)	11 ($A.B$)	10 ($A.\overline{B}$)
0($\overline{C}$)	$\overline{A}.\overline{B}.\overline{C}$	$\overline{A}.B.\overline{C}$	$A.B.\overline{C}$	$A.\overline{B}.\overline{C}$
1(C)	$\overline{A}.\overline{B}.C$	$\overline{A}.B.C$	$A.B.C$	$A.\overline{B}.C$

(b)

C \ A.B	00	01	11	10
0	0	0	1	0
1	1	1	0	0

(c)

(ii) To simplify a three-variable Boolean expression, the Boolean expression is depicted on a Karnaugh map as outlined above. Any cells on the map having common edges either vertically or horizontally are grouped together to form couples of four cells or two cells. During coupling the horizontal lines at the top and bottom of the cells are taken as a common edge, as are the vertical lines on the left and right of the cells. The simplified Boolean expression for a couple is given by those variables common to all cells in the couple.

(iii) A horizontal couple may be formed as shown by the broken line in *Table 5*. The variables common to each cell of the couple are $A = 0$, i.e., $\overline{A}$, and $C = 1$, i.e. C. Thus the two terms represented by the couple, $\overline{A}.\overline{B}.C + \overline{A}.B.C$ are equivalent to $\overline{A}.C$. Hence the Boolean expression $\overline{A}.\overline{B}.C + \overline{A}.B.C + A.B.\overline{C}$

Table 5

C \ A.B	00	01	11	10
0	0	0	1	0
1	1	1	0	0

simplifies to $\overline{A}.C + A.B.\overline{C}$, the latter term representing the 1 in the third column of the top row.

4 Four-variable Karnaugh maps

(i) A truth table for a four-variable expression is shown in *Table 6(a)*, the 1's in the output column showing that:

$$Z = \overline{A}.\overline{B}.C.\overline{D} + \overline{A}.B.C.\overline{D} + A.\overline{B}.C.\overline{D} + A.B.C.\overline{D}.$$

Each of the sixteen possible Boolean expressions associated with a four-variable function can be depicted as shown in *Table 6(b)*, in which one cell is allocated to each row of the truth table. A matrix similar to that shown in *Table 6(b)* can be used to depict

$$Z = \overline{A}.\overline{B}.C.\overline{D} + \overline{A}.B.C.\overline{D} + A.\overline{B}.C.\overline{D} + A.B.C.\overline{D},$$

by putting 1's in the cells corresponding to the Boolean terms on the right of the Boolean equation and 0's in the remaining cells. This method of depicting a four-variable expression is called a four-variable Karnaugh map, and is shown in *Table 6(c)*.

(ii) To simplify a four-variable Boolean expression, the Boolean expression is depicted on a Karnaugh map as outlined above. Any cells on the map having common edges either vertically or horizontally are grouped together to form couples of eight cells, four cells or two cells. During coupling, the horizontal lines at the top and bottom of the cells may be considered to be common edges, as are the vertical lines on the left and the right of the cells. The simplified Boolean expression for a couple is given by those variables common to all cells in the couple.

(iii) A horizontal couple may be formed by the four 1's in the bottom row of *Table 6(c)*. The only variables common to all the cells in the couple are C and $\overline{D}$. Hence the minimised expression of

$$\overline{A}.\overline{B}.C.\overline{D} + \overline{A}B.C.\overline{D} + A.\overline{B}.C.\overline{D} + A.B.C.\overline{D} \text{ is } C.\overline{D}$$

(which may be checked using the laws and rules of Boolean algebra).

Table 6

| Inputs | | | | Output | Boolean |
A	B	C	D	Z	expression
0	0	0	0	0	$\bar{A}.\bar{B}.\bar{C}.\bar{D}$
0	0	0	1	0	$\bar{A}.\bar{B}.\bar{C}.D$
0	0	1	0	1	$\bar{A}.\bar{B}.C.\bar{D}$
0	0	1	1	0	$\bar{A}.\bar{B}.C.D$
0	1	0	0	0	$\bar{A}.B.\bar{C}.\bar{D}$
0	1	0	1	0	$\bar{A}.B.\bar{C}.D$
0	1	1	0	1	$\bar{A}.B.C.\bar{D}$
0	1	1	1	0	$\bar{A}.B.C.D$
1	0	0	0	0	$A.\bar{B}.\bar{C}.\bar{D}$
1	0	0	1	0	$A.\bar{B}.\bar{C}.D$
1	0	1	0	1	$A.\bar{B}.C.\bar{D}$
1	0	1	1	0	$A.\bar{B}.C.D$
1	1	0	0	0	$A.B.\bar{C}.\bar{D}$
1	1	0	1	0	$A.B.\bar{C}.D$
1	1	1	0	1	$A.B.C.\bar{D}$
1	1	1	1	0	$A.B.C.D$

(a)

A.B \ C.D	00 ($\bar{A}.\bar{B}$)	01 ($\bar{A}.B$)	11 ($A.B$)	10 ($A.\bar{B}$)
00 ($\bar{C}.\bar{D}$)	$\bar{A}.\bar{B}.\bar{C}.\bar{D}$	$\bar{A}.B.\bar{C}.\bar{D}$	$A.B.\bar{C}.\bar{D}$	$A.\bar{B}.\bar{C}.\bar{D}$
01 ($\bar{C}.D$)	$\bar{A}.\bar{B}.\bar{C}.D$	$\bar{A}.B.\bar{C}.D$	$A.B.\bar{C}.D$	$A.\bar{B}.\bar{C}.D$
11 ($C.D$)	$\bar{A}.\bar{B}.C.D$	$\bar{A}.B.C.D$	$A.B.C.D$	$A.\bar{B}.C.D$
10 ($C.\bar{D}$)	$\bar{A}.\bar{B}.C.\bar{D}$	$\bar{A}.B.C.\bar{D}$	$A.B.C.\bar{D}$	$A.\bar{B}.C.\bar{D}$

(b)

A.B \ C.D	0.0	0.1	1.1	1.0
0.0	0	0	0	0
0.1	0	0	0	0
1.1	0	0	0	0
1.0	1	1	1	1

(c)

5 Summary of procedure when simplifying a Boolean expression using a Karnaugh map

(a) Draw a four, eight or sixteen-cell matrix, depending on whether there are two, three or four variables.

(b) Mark in the Boolean expression by putting 1's in the appropriate cells.

(c) Form couples of 8, 4 or 2 cells having common edges, forming the largest

groups of cells possible. (Note that a cell containing a 1 may be used more than once when forming a couple. Also note that each cell containing a 1 must be used at least once.)
(d) The Boolean expression for a couple is given by the variables which are common to all cells in the couple.

B WORKED PROBLEMS ON THE SIMPLIFICATION OF BOOLEAN EXPRESSIONS USING KARNAUGH MAPS

Problem 1 Use Karnaugh map techniques to simplify the expression $\overline{P}.\overline{Q} + \overline{P}.Q$.

Using the procedure given in para. 5,
(a) the two-variable matrix is drawn and is shown in *Table 7*,
(b) The term $\overline{P}.\overline{Q}$ is marked with a 1 in the top left-hand cell, corresponding to $P = 0$ and $Q = 0$. $\overline{P}.Q$ is marked with a 1 in the bottom left-hand cell corresponding to $P = 0$ and $Q = 1$.

Table 7

(c) The two cells containing 1's have a common horizontal edge and thus a vertical couple, shown by the broken line, can be formed.
(d) The variable common to both cells in the couple is $P = 0$, i.e. $\overline{P}$, thus $\overline{P}.\overline{Q} + \overline{P}.Q = \overline{P}$.

Problem 2 Simplify the Boolean expression $X.\overline{Y} + X.Y + \overline{X}.Y$ by using a Karnaugh map.

Using the procedure given in para. 5,
(a) a two variable matrix is drawn as shown in *Table 8*.
(b) the term $X.\overline{Y}$ is marked with a 1 in the top right-hand cell, corresponding to $X = 1$ and $Y = 0$. $X.Y$ is marked with a 1 in the bottom right-hand cell,

Table 8

corresponding to $X = 1$ and $Y = 1$. $\overline{X}.Y$ is marked with a 1 in the bottom left-hand cell, corresponding to $X = 0$ and $Y = 1$.
(c) Couples are formed from (i) the two vertical cells $X.\overline{Y}$ and $X.Y$, and (ii) the two horizontal cells $\overline{X}.Y$ and $X.Y$, the couples being shown by broken lines.
(d) The only variable common to couple (i) is X and that common to couple (ii) is Y. Thus $X.\overline{Y} + X.Y + \overline{X}.Y$ simplifies to $X + Y$.

Problem 3 Simplify the expression

$$\bar{X}.Y.\bar{Z} + \bar{X}.\bar{Y}.Z + X.Y.\bar{Z} + X.\bar{Y}.Z$$

by using Karnaugh map techniques.

Using the procedure given in para. 5,
(a) a three-variable matrix is drawn and is shown in *Table 9*,
(b) the 1's on the matrix correspond to the expression given, i.e., for $\bar{X}.Y.\bar{Z}$, $X=0$, $Y=1$ and $Z=0$ and hence corresponds to the cell in the top row and second column, and so on.

Table 9

X.Y \ Z	0.0	0.1	1.1	1.0
0	0	1	1	0
1	1	1	0	0	1

(c) Two couples can be formed, shown by the broken lines. The couple in the bottom row may be formed since the vertical lines on the left and right of the cells are taken as a common edge.
(d) The variables common to the couple in the top row are $Y=1$ and $Z=0$, that is, $Y.\bar{Z}$ and the variables common to the couple in the bottom row are $Y=0$, $Z=1$, that is, $\bar{Y}.Z$. Hence:

$$\bar{X}.Y.\bar{Z} + \bar{X}\bar{Y}.Z + X.Y.\bar{Z} + X.\bar{Y}.Z = Y.\bar{Z} + \bar{Y}.Z$$

Problem 4 Determine the minimised expression for the Boolean function:

$$A.B.C. + A.\bar{B}.C + A.\bar{B}.\bar{C} + A.B.\bar{C}$$

by using (i) the laws and rules of Boolean algebra and (ii) Karnaugh map techniques. Prove the result by using a truth table.

(i) Using the laws and rules of Boolean algebra (see *Table 1*):

		Reference
$A.B.C + A.\bar{B}.C + A.\bar{B}.\bar{C} + A.B.\bar{C}$	$= A.C(B+\bar{B}) + A.\bar{C}(B+\bar{B})$	(5)
	$= A.C.1 + A.\bar{C}.1$	(10)
	$= A.C. + A.\bar{C}$	(12)
	$= A.(C+\bar{C})$	(5)
	$= A.1$	(10)
	$= A$	(12)

(Further worked problems showing how Boolean expressions are simplified using the laws and rules of Boolean algebra may be found in Chapter 4 of *Digital Techniques 2 Checkbook*.)

(ii) Using the procedure given in para 5,
(a) a three-variable matrix is drawn as shown in *Table 10(a)*.

Table 10

(a)

C \ A.B	00	01	11	10
0	0	0	1	1
1	0	0	1	1

(b)

A	B	C	OUTPUT	
0	0	0	0	
0	0	1	0	
0	1	0	0	
0	1	1	0	
1	0	0	1	$(A.\bar{B}.\bar{C})$
1	0	1	1	$(A.\bar{B}.C)$
1	1	0	1	$(A.B.\bar{C})$
1	1	1	1	$(A.B.C)$

(b) The 1's on the matrix corresponds to the given expression. For example, $A.B.C$, i.e. $A=1$, $B=1$ and $C=1$ corresponds to the cell in the bottom row and third column.

(c) A four-cell couple is formed as shown by the broken lines in *Table 10(a)*.

(d) The only variable common to the couple is $A = 1$.

Hence the Boolean expression $A.B.C + A.\bar{B}.C + A.\bar{B}.\bar{C} + A.B.\bar{C}$ simplifies to A as in part (i). A truth table representing the given Boolean expression is shown in *Table 10(b)*. Since the output column, corresponding to $A.B.C + A.\bar{B}.C + A.\bar{B}.\bar{C} + A.B.\bar{C}$, is the same as input column A, then the Boolean expression simplifies to A.

Problem 5 Simplify $A.\bar{C} + \bar{A}.(B+C) + A.B.(C+\bar{B})$ using (i) the rules of Boolean algebra and (ii) Karnaugh map techniques.

(i) The rules of Boolean algebra are given in *Table 1*, page 1.

Reference

$$\begin{aligned}
A.\bar{C} + \bar{A}.(B+C) + A.B.(C+\bar{B}) &= A.\bar{C} + \bar{A}.B + \bar{A}.C + A.B.C + A.B.\bar{B} & (5) \\
&= A.\bar{C} + \bar{A}.B + \bar{A}.C + A.B.C + A.O & (14) \\
&= A.\bar{C} + \bar{A}.B + \bar{A}.C + A.B.C & (11) \ldots (1) \\
&= A.(\bar{C} + B.C.) + \bar{A}.B + \bar{A}.C & (5) \\
&= A.(\bar{C} + B) + \bar{A}.B + \bar{A}.C & (17) \\
&= A.\bar{C} + A.B + \bar{A}.B + \bar{A}.C & (5) \\
&= A.\bar{C} + B.(A + \bar{A}) + \bar{A}.C & (5) \\
&= A.\bar{C} + B.1 + \bar{A}.C & (10) \\
&= A.\bar{C} + B + \bar{A}.C & (12)
\end{aligned}$$

(ii) (a) A 3-variable matrix is drawn as shown in *Table 11*.

(b) If a Boolean expression contains brackets it is often easier to remove them, using the laws and rules of Boolean algebra, before plotting the function on a Karnaugh map. The expression is thus simplified to equation (1) in part (i).

By law 5 of *Table 1*, of page 1: $A.\overline{C}$ can be re-written as $A.\overline{C}.(B + \overline{B})$ i.e., $A.B.\overline{C} + A.\overline{B}.\overline{C}$. These terms are plotted on the Karnaugh map in the two right hand cells in the top row, corresponding to 110 and 100. Similarly $\overline{A}.B$ is equivalent to $\overline{A}.B.(C + \overline{C})$ or $\overline{A}.B.C + \overline{A}.B.\overline{C}$ corresponding to 011 and 010 which are plotted in each of the two cells in the second column of *Table 11*. Each of the other terms are plotted on the Karnaugh map as shown.

Table 11

C \ A.B	00	01	11	10
0	0	1	1	1
1	1	1	1	0

(c) A 4-cell couple and two 2-cell couples are formed as shown by the broken lines.
(d) The only variable common to the 4-cell couple is $B = 1$, i.e. B. The variables common to the 2-cell couple on the top right of the map is $A = 1$ and $C = 0$, i.e. $A.\overline{C}$.

The variables common to the 2-cell couple on the bottom left of the map is $A = 0$ and $C = 1$, i.e. $\overline{A}.C$.

Thus $A.\overline{C} + \overline{A}.(B + C) + A.B.(C + \overline{B})$ simplifies to $B + A.\overline{C} + \overline{A}.C$, as obtained in part (i).

Problem 6 Produce the minimised expression for the output given in the truth table shown in *Table 12* by using Karnaugh map techniques.

Table 12

A	B	C	OUTPUT
0	0	0	1
0	0	1	0
0	1	0	0
0	1	1	0
1	0	0	1
1	0	1	1
1	1	0	1
1	1	1	1

Table 13

C \ A.B	00	01	11	10
0	1	0	1	1
1	0	0	1	1

The output of the truth table represents the Boolean expression:

$$\overline{A}.\overline{B}.\overline{C} + A.\overline{B}.\overline{C} + A.\overline{B}.C + A.B.\overline{C} + A.B.C$$

(a) A 3-variable matrix is drawn as shown in *Table 13*.
(b) The 1's on the matrix correspond to the given expression. For example, $\overline{A}.\overline{B}.\overline{C}$ corresponds to 000, which is shown by a 1 in the top left-hand cell.

Similarly, $A.\overline{B}.\overline{C}$ corresponds to 100, which is shown by a 1 in the top right-hand cell, and so on.

(c) Two couples can be formed, a 4-cell couple and a 2-cell couple as shown by the broken lines. The vertical edges on the left and right of the map are considered to have a common edge.

(d) The only variable common to all four cells of the 4-cell couple is $A = 1$, i.e. A. The variable common to the 2-cell couple are $B = 0$ and $C = 0$, i.e. $\overline{B}\overline{C}$.

Thus the output given in the truth table of *Table 12* simplifies to $A + \overline{B}.\overline{C}$.

Problem 7 Use a Karnaugh map technique to simplify the expression $\overline{(\overline{A}.B)}.(\overline{A} + B)$.

Using the procedure given in para. 5, a two-variable matrix is drawn and is shown in *Table 14*.

Table 14

B \ A	0	1
0	1	1 2
1		1

$\overline{A}.B$ corresponds to the bottom left-hand cell and $\overline{(\overline{A}.B)}$ must therefore be all cells except this one, marked with a 1 in *Table 14*. $(\overline{A} + B)$ corresponds to all the cells except the top right-hand cell marked with a 2 in *Table 14*. Hence $\overline{(\overline{A} + B)}$ must correspond to the cell marked with a 2. The expression $\overline{(\overline{A}.B)}.\overline{(\overline{A} + B)}$ corresponds to the cell having both 1 and 2 in it,

i.e., $\overline{(\overline{A}.B)}.\overline{(\overline{A}+B)} = A.\overline{B}$.

Problem 8 Simplify $\overline{(P + \overline{Q}.R)} + \overline{(P.Q + \overline{R})}$ using a Karnaugh map technique.

The term $(P + \overline{Q}.R)$ corresponds to the cells marked 1 on the matrix in *Table 15(a)*, hence $\overline{(P + \overline{Q}.R)}$ corresponds to the cells marked 2. Similarly $(P.Q + \overline{R})$ corresponds to the cells marked 3 in *Table 15(a)*, hence $\overline{(P.Q + \overline{R})}$ corresponds to the cells marked 4. The expression $\overline{(P + \overline{Q}.R)} + \overline{(P.Q + \overline{R})}$ corresponds to cells marked with either a 2 or with a 4 and is shown in *Table 15(b)* by X's.

Table 15

R \ P.Q	0.0	0.1	1.1	1.0
0	3 2	3 2	3 1	3 1
1	4 1	4 2	3 1	4 1

(a)

R \ P.Q	0.0	0.1	1.1	1.0
0	X	X		
1	X	X		X

(b)

These cells may be coupled as shown by the broken lines. The variables common to the group of four cells is $P = 0$, i.e., $\overline{P}$, and those common to the group of two cells are $Q = 0$, $R = 1$, i.e., $\overline{Q}.R$. Thus:

$$(\overline{P+\overline{Q}.R})+(\overline{P.Q.+\overline{R}})=\overline{P}+\overline{Q}.R$$

Problem 9 Use Karnaugh map techniques to simplify the expression:

$$A.B.\overline{C}.\overline{D}+A.B.C.D+\overline{A}.B.C.D+A.B.C.\overline{D}+\overline{A}.B.C.\overline{D}$$

Using the procedure given in para. 5, a four-variable matrix is drawn and is shown in *Table 16*. The 1's marked on the matrix correspond to the expression given. Two couples can be formed and are shown by the broken lines. The four-cell couple has $B = 1$, $C = 1$, i.e., $B.C$ as the common variables to all four cells and the two-cell couple has $A.B.\overline{D}$ as the common variable to both cells. Hence, the expression simplifies to:

$B.C.+A.B.\overline{D}$, i.e. $B.(C+A.\overline{D})$

Table 16

A.B C.D	0.0	0.1	1.1	1.0
0.0			1	
0.1				
1.1		1	1	
1.0		1	1	

Problem 10 Simplify the expression

$$\overline{A}.\overline{B}.\overline{C}.\overline{D}+A.\overline{B}.\overline{C}.\overline{D}+\overline{A}.\overline{B}.C.\overline{D}+A.\overline{B}.C.\overline{D}+A.B.C.D$$

by using Karnaugh map techniques.

The Karnaugh map for the expression given is shown in *Table 17*. Since the top and bottom horizontal lines are common edges and the vertical lines on the left and right of the cells are common, then the four corner cells form a couple, $\overline{B}.\overline{D}$ (the cells can be considered as if they are stretched to completely cover a sphere, as far as common edges are concerned). The cell $A.B.C.D$ cannot be coupled with any other. Hence the expression simplifies to $\overline{B}.\overline{D} + A.B.C.D$.

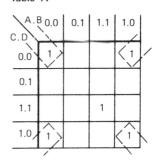

Table 17

11

Problem 11 Use a Karnaugh map to produce the minimised expression for the Boolean function given by:

$$A.B.\overline{C}.\overline{D}+\overline{A}.\overline{B}.\overline{C}.\overline{D}+\overline{A}.B.C.D+ \overline{A}.\overline{B}.C.D+A.\overline{B}.\overline{C}.\overline{D}+ \overline{A}.\overline{B}.C.\overline{D}+\overline{A}.B.C.\overline{D}$$

The Karnaugh map for the given expression is shown in *Table 18*. A 4-cell couple and three 2-cell couple are formed as shown.

Table 18

A.B C.D	00	01	11	10
00	1		1	1
01				
11	1	1		
10	1	1		

The variables common to the 4-cell couple are $A = 0$ nd $C = 1$, i.e. $\overline{A}.C$.
The variables common to the 2-cell couple formed by the two cells on the far right of the top row are $A = 1$, $C = 0$ and $D = 0$, i.e. $A.\overline{C}.\overline{D}$
The variables common to the 2-cell couple formed by the cells on the far left and far right of the top row are $B = 0$, $C = 0$ and $D = 0$, i.e. $\overline{B}.\overline{C}.\overline{D}$

The variables common to the 2-cell couple formed by the cells at the top and bottom of the first column are $A = 0$, $B = 0$ and $D = 0$, i.e. $\overline{A}.\overline{B}.\overline{D}$
Hence the minimised expression for the Boolean function is:

$$\overline{A}.C+A.\overline{C}.\overline{D}+\overline{B}.\overline{C}.\overline{D}+\overline{A}.\overline{B}.\overline{D}$$

or $\overline{A}.C+A.\overline{C}.\overline{D}+ \overline{B}.\overline{D}.(\overline{A}+\overline{C})$

C. FURTHER PROBLEMS ON THE SIMPLIFICATION OF BOOLEAN EXPRESSIONS USING KARNAUGH MAPS

In Problems 1 to 6 use Karnaugh map techniques to simplify the expressions given.

1. $\overline{A}.\overline{B}+A.\overline{B}$ $[\overline{B}]$
2. $\overline{A}.\overline{B}+A.\overline{B}+\overline{A}.B$ $[\overline{A}+\overline{B}]$
1. $\overline{X}.Y+X.Y$ $[Y]$
4. $\overline{X}.\overline{Y}+X.\overline{Y}+X.Y$ $[X+\overline{Y}]$
5. $\overline{A}.\overline{B}+\overline{A}.B+A.B$ $[\overline{A}+B]$
6. $(\overline{P}.\overline{Q}).(\overline{\overline{P}.Q})$ $[\overline{P}.\overline{Q}]$

7. Simplify the Boolean expression corresponding to the output of the truth table shown in *Table 19*. $[\overline{A}]$

In *Problems 8 to 16*, produce the minimised expression for the Boolean functions given.

8. $\overline{A}.\overline{B}.\overline{C}+\overline{A}.\overline{B}.C+A.B.\overline{C}+ A.\overline{B}.\overline{C}+A.\overline{B}.C$ $[\overline{B}+A.\overline{C}]$

Table 19

A	B	OUTPUT
0	0	1
0	1	1
1	0	0
1	1	0

Table 20

P	Q	R	OUTPUT
0	0	0	1
0	0	1	0
0	1	0	0
0	1	1	1
1	0	0	1
1	0	1	0
1	1	0	0
1	1	1	1

9 $A.B.\overline{C} + \overline{A}.\overline{B}.\overline{C} + \overline{A}.B.\overline{C} + A.\overline{B}.\overline{C}$ $[\overline{C}]$

10 $\overline{P}.\overline{Q}.\overline{R} + P.Q.\overline{R} + P.Q.R. + \overline{P}.\overline{R}$ $[P.Q. + \overline{P}.\overline{R}]$

11 $\overline{A}.B.C + A.C + \overline{B}.C$ $[C]$

12 $\overline{P}.\overline{Q}.\overline{R} + \overline{P}.Q.\overline{R} + P.Q.\overline{R}$ $[\overline{R}.(\overline{P} + Q)]$

13 $\overline{P}.\overline{Q}.\overline{R} + P.Q.\overline{R} + P.Q.R + P.\overline{Q}.R$ $[P.(Q + R) + \overline{P}.\overline{Q}.\overline{R}]$

14 $(\overline{X.Y} + Z) + \overline{(X + \overline{Y.Z})}$ $[\overline{X} + \overline{Y} + Z]$

15 $(\overline{\overline{X}.Z + X.Y.Z}).(\overline{X.\overline{Y}})$ $[\overline{Z}.(\overline{X} + Y)]$

16 $\overline{(\overline{X}.Y + \overline{X}.Z)} + (X.Y.Z)$ $[X + \overline{Y} + \overline{Z}]$

17 Simplify the Boolean expression corresponding to the output of the truth table shown in *Table 20*. $[Q.R + \overline{Q}.\overline{R}]$

18 Repeat *Problems 1 to 13* using the laws and rules of Boolean algebra.

19 $\overline{A}.\overline{B}.\overline{C}.\overline{D} + \overline{A}.B.\overline{C.D} + \overline{A}.B.\overline{C}.D$ $[\overline{A}.\overline{C}.(B + \overline{D})]$

20 $\overline{A}.\overline{B}.C.D. + \overline{A}.\overline{B}.C.\overline{D} + A.\overline{B}.C.\overline{D}$ $[\overline{B}.C.(\overline{A} + \overline{D})]$

21 $\overline{A}.B.\overline{C}.D + A.B.\overline{C}.D + A.B.C.D + A.\overline{B}.\overline{C}.D + A.\overline{B}.C.D.$ $[D.(A + B.\overline{C})]$

22 $A.B.C.D. + A.\overline{B}.C.D. + A.B.C.\overline{D} + A.\overline{B}.C.\overline{D} + \overline{A}.\overline{B}.C.D$ $[A.C. + \overline{B}.C.D]$

23 $\overline{A}.\overline{B}.\overline{C}.D + A.B.\overline{C}.\overline{D} + A.\overline{B}.\overline{C}.\overline{D} + A.B.C.\overline{D} + A.\overline{B}.C.\overline{D}$ $[A.\overline{D} + \overline{A}.\overline{B}.\overline{C}.D]$

2 Logic Circuits

A MAIN POINTS CONCERNED WITH LOGIC CIRCUITS

1 Simplification of Boolean expressions can be achieved using the laws and rules of Boolean algebra (see *Table 1*, page 1) or by using Karnaugh map techniques (see chapter 1). A third method of minimisation of Boolean expressions is by applying **de Morgan's laws,** which are used extensively in logic circuit design.

2 De Morgan's laws may be used to simplify **not**-functions having two or more elements. The laws state that:

$$\overline{A + B} = \overline{A}.\overline{B} \qquad (1)$$
$$\overline{A.B} = \overline{A} + \overline{B} \qquad (2)$$

and may be verified by using truth tables (see *Problems 1 and 2*). The rules governing the application of de Morgan's laws are:
   (i)   invert the variables — in law (i), $\overline{A + B}$ becomes $\overline{A} + \overline{B}$
   (ii) change the connections — i.e., change + to . (or vice versa) thus $\overline{A} + \overline{B}$ becomes $\overline{A}.\overline{B}$, and
   (iii) invert the whole expression — i.e., $\overline{\overline{A}.\overline{B}}$ becomes $\overline{\overline{A}.\overline{B}}$ which is the same as $\overline{A}.\overline{B}$ (from law 18 of *Table 1,* page 1).

Applying these rules to law (2):

(i) $A.B$ becomes $\overline{\overline{A}.\overline{B}}$ (ii) $\overline{\overline{A}.\overline{B}}$ becomes $\overline{\overline{A} + \overline{B}}$

(iii) $\overline{\overline{A} + \overline{B}}$ becomes $\overline{\overline{A} + \overline{B}}$, which is $\overline{A} + \overline{B}$.

Since de Morgan's laws produce the equivalent of any expression to which they are applied, it is possible to apply them to any part of, or the whole of an expression. (See *Problems 3 to 7*.)

3 In practice, logic gates are used to perform the **AND, OR** and **NOT**-functions introduced in chapter 4 of *Digital Techniques 2 Checkbook*. Logic gates can be made from switches, magnetic devices or fluidic devices, but most logic gates in use are electronic devices. Various logic gates are available. For example, the Boolean expression $(A.B.C)$ can be produced using a three-input, **AND**-gate and $(C + D)$ by using a two-input **OR**-gate. The principal gates in common use are introduced in paras. 4 to 8. The term "gate" is used in the same sense as a normal gate, the open state being indicated by a binary "1" and the closed state by a binary "0". A gate will open only when the requirements of the gate are met and, for example, there will only be a "1" output on a two-input **AND**-gate when both the inputs to the gate are at a "1" state.

4 **The AND-gate** Two different symbols used for a three-input, **AND**-gate are shown in *Fig 1(a)* and the truth table is shown in *Fig 1(b)*. This shows that there will only be a "1" output when A is 1 and B is 1 and C is 1, written as:

$Z = A.B.C.$

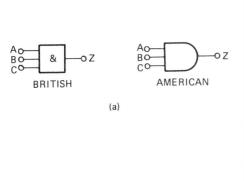

Fig 1

5. **The OR-gate** Two different symbols used for a three-input **OR**-gate are shown in *Fig 2(a)* and the truth table is shown in *Fig 2(b)*. This shows that there will be a "1" output when A is 1, or B is 1, or C is 1, or any combinations of A, B or C is 1, written as

$$Z = A + B + C.$$

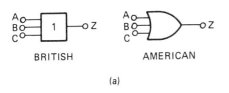

Fig 2

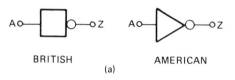

Fig 3

6. **The invert-gate or NOT-gate** Two different symbols used for an **invert**-gate are shown in *Fig 3(a)* and the truth table is shown in *Fig 3(b)*. This shows that a "0" input gives a "1" output and vice versa, i.e. it is an "opposite to" function. The invert of A is written $\overline{A}$ and is called "**NOT-**A".

7. **The NAND-gate** Two different symbols used for a **NAND**-gate are shown in *Fig 4(a)* and the truth table is shown in *Fig 4(b)*. This gate is equivalent to an **AND**-gate and an **invert**-gate in series (not-and = nand) and the output is written as

   $$Z = \overline{A.B.C}.$$

8. The **NOR**-gate Two different symbols used for a **NOR**-gate are shown in *Fig 5(a)* and the truth table is shown in *Fig 5(b)*. This gate is equivalent to an **OR**-gate and an **invert**-gate in series (NOR-OR = NOR), and the output is written as

   $$Z = \overline{A + B + C}.$$

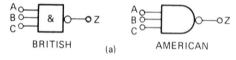

INPUTS				OUTPUT
A	B	C	A.B.C.	$Z = \overline{A.B.C.}$
0	0	0	0	1
0	0	1	0	1
0	1	0	0	1
0	1	1	0	1
1	0	0	0	1
1	0	1	0	1
1	1	0	0	1
1	1	1	1	0

(b)   **Fig 4**

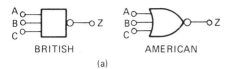

BRITISH　　　　　　AMERICAN

(a)

INPUTS				OUTPUT
A	B	C	A+B+C	Z=$\overline{A+B+C}$
0	0	0	0	1
0	0	1	1	0
0	1	0	1	0
0	1	1	1	0
1	0	0	1	0
1	0	1	1	0
1	1	0	1	0
1	1	1	1	0

(b)　　　　　　　　Fig 5

9 **Combinational logic networks** In most logic circuits, more than one gate is needed to give the required output. Except for the **invert**-gate, logic gates generally have two, three or four inputs and are confined to one function only, thus, for example, a two-input, **OR**-gate or a four-input **AND**-gate can be used when designing a logic circuit. They way in which logic gates are used to generate a given output is shown in *Problems 8 to 11*.

10 **Universal logic gates** The function of any of the five logic gates in common use can be obtained by using either **NAND**-gates or **NOR**-gates and when used in this manner, the gate selected is called a **universal gate**.

Logic gates may be obtained reasonably inexpensively as integrated circuits; one integrated circuit chip usually containing several logic gates. The majority of integrated circuit gates that are used belong to either the TTL or CMOS families (see chapter 3). In each of these families, **NAND** or **NOR**-gates are the most commonly used since their cost is less than other types of gates. In addition, **NAND** and **NOR**-gates generally have a faster operating speed and a lower power dissipation than other gates. Thus digital circuits are often made up using on **NAND** and/or **NOR**-gates. Problems involving universal NAND and NOR logic may be found in *Problems 12 to 25*.

B WORKED PROBLEMS ON LOGIC CIRCUITS

Problem 1. Verify de Morgan's law: $\overline{A + B} = \overline{A}.\overline{B}$ by using a truth table.

In *Table 1*, columns 1 and 2 give all the possible arrangements of the inputs A and B. Column 3 is the **OR**-function applied to columns 1 and 2 and column 4

Table 1

1 A	2 B	3 A+B	4 $\overline{A+B}$	5 $\overline{A}$	6 $\overline{B}$	7 $\overline{A}.\overline{B}$
0	0	0	1	1	1	1
0	1	1	0	1	0	0
1	0	1	0	0	1	0
1	1	1	0	0	0	0

is the **NOT**-function applied to column 3. Columns 5 and 6 are the **NOT**-function applied to columns 1 and 2 respectively and column 7 is the **AND**-function applied to columns 5 and 6.

Since columns 4 and 7 have the same pattern of 0's and 1's this verifies that $\overline{A + B} = \overline{A}.\overline{B}$.

Problem 2 Use a truth table to verify de Morgan's law: $\overline{A.B} = \overline{A} + \overline{B}$.

In *Table 2*, columns 1 and 2 give all the possible arrangements of the inputs A and B. Column 3 is the **AND**-function applied to columns 1 and 2 and column 4 is the **NOT**-function applied to column 3. Columns 5 and 6 are the **NOT**-

Table 2

1 A	2 B	3 A.B	4 $\overline{A.B}$	5 $\overline{A}$	6 $\overline{B}$	7 $\overline{A}+\overline{B}$
0	0	0	1	1	1	1
0	1	0	1	1	0	1
1	0	0	1	0	1	1
1	1	1	0	0	0	0

functions applied to columns 1 and 2 respectively and column 7 is the **OR**-function applied to columns 5 and 6. Since columns 4 and 7 have the same pattern of 0's and 1's this verifies that $\overline{A.B} = \overline{A} + \overline{B}$.

Problem 3 Simplify the Boolean expression $(\overline{\overline{A}.B}) + (\overline{\overline{A} + B})$ by using de Morgan's law and the rules of Boolean algebra.

18

Applying de Morgan's law (2) (see para. 2) to the first term gives:

$\overline{\overline{A}.B} = \overline{\overline{A}} + \overline{B} = A + \overline{B}$, since $\overline{\overline{A}} = A$.

Applying de Morgan's law (1) to the second term gives:

$\overline{\overline{A} + B} = \overline{\overline{A}}.\overline{B} = A.\overline{B}$

Thus, $(\overline{\overline{A}.B}) + (\overline{\overline{A} + B}) = (A + \overline{B}) + A.\overline{B}$

Removing the bracket and reordering gives: $A + A.\overline{B} + \overline{B}$

But by rule 15, *Table 1*, page 1, $A + A.B = A$. It follows that: $A + A.\overline{B} = A$
Thus: $(\overline{\overline{A}.B}) + (\overline{\overline{A} + B}) = A + \overline{B}$.

Problem 4 Simplify the Boolean expression $(\overline{\overline{A}.B}).(\overline{\overline{A} + B})$ using de Morgan's law and the laws and rules of Boolean algebra.

(This is the same problem as *Problem 7* of chapter 1, which was simplified using Karnaugh maps.)

By de Morgan's law (2), $(\overline{\overline{A}.B}) = \overline{\overline{A}} + \overline{B} = A + \overline{B}$ by law 18 of *Table 1*, page 1
By de Morgan's law (1), $(\overline{\overline{A} + B}) = \overline{\overline{A}}.\overline{B} = A.\overline{B}$

Hence $(\overline{\overline{A}.B}).(\overline{\overline{A} + B}) = (A + \overline{B}).(A.\overline{B}) = A.A.\overline{B} + \overline{B}.A.\overline{B}$ by law 5
$= A.\overline{B} + A.\overline{B}$ by law 13
$= A.\overline{B}$ by law 9.

Problem 5 Simplify $(\overline{P + \overline{Q}.R}) + (\overline{P.Q + \overline{R}})$ using de Morgan's laws and the laws and rules of Boolean algebra.

(This is the same as *Problem 8* of chapter 1 which was simplified using Karnaugh maps.)

By de Morgan's law (1), $(\overline{P+\overline{Q}.R}) = \overline{P}.\overline{\overline{Q}.R}$
By de Morgan's law (2), $\overline{\overline{Q}.R} = \overline{\overline{Q}} + \overline{R} = Q + \overline{R}$

Hence $(\overline{P+\overline{Q}.R}) = \overline{P}(Q+\overline{R}) = \overline{P}.Q + \overline{P}.\overline{R}$
By de Morgan's law (1), $(\overline{P.Q. + \overline{R}}) = \overline{P.Q}.\overline{\overline{R}} = \overline{P.Q}.R$
By de Morgan's law (2), $\overline{P.Q}.R = (\overline{P}+\overline{Q}).R = \overline{P}.R + \overline{Q}.R$

Hence $(\overline{P+Q.R}) + (\overline{P.Q + \overline{R}}) = \overline{P}.Q + \overline{P}.\overline{R} + \overline{P}.R + \overline{Q}.R$
$= \overline{P}.Q + \overline{P}.(\overline{R} + R) + \overline{Q}.R$ by law 5 of *Table 1*, page 1
$= \overline{P}.Q + \overline{P}.1 + \overline{Q}.R$ by law 10
$= \overline{P}.(Q + 1) + \overline{Q}.R$ by law 5
$= \overline{P}.1 + \overline{Q}.R$ by law 8
$= \overline{P} + \overline{Q}.R$ by law 12

Problem 6 Simplify the Boolean expression $\overline{(A.\overline{B}+C)}.\overline{(\overline{A}+B.\overline{C})}$ by using de Morgan's laws and the rules of Boolean algebra.

Applying de Morgan's law (1), (see para. 2), to the first term gives:
$$\overline{A.\overline{B}+C} = \overline{A.\overline{B}}.\overline{C} = (\overline{A}+\overline{\overline{B}}).\overline{C}$$
$$= (\overline{A}+B).\overline{C} = \overline{A}.C + B.\overline{C}$$

Applying de Morgan's law (1) to the second term gives:
$$\overline{\overline{A}+B.\overline{C}} = A + (\overline{B}+C)$$

Thus $\overline{(A.\overline{B}+C)}.\overline{(\overline{A}+B.\overline{C})} = (\overline{A}.C + B.\overline{C}).(\overline{A}+\overline{B}+C)$
$$= \overline{A}.\overline{A}.C + \overline{A}.\overline{B}.C + \overline{A}.\overline{C}.C + \overline{A}.B.\overline{C} + B.\overline{B}.\overline{C} + B.\overline{C}.C$$

But from *Table 1,* page 1, $\overline{A}.\overline{A} = \overline{A}$ and $\overline{C}.C = B.\overline{B} = 0$

Hence the Boolean expression becomes $\overline{A}.C + \overline{A}.\overline{B}.C + \overline{A}.B.\overline{C}$
The first two terms are of the form $P + P.Q = P$, where $\overline{A}.C \equiv P$ and $\overline{B} \equiv Q$,
giving $\overline{A}.C + \overline{A}.B.\overline{C}$, i.e., $\overline{A}.(C + B.\overline{C})$
But from *Table 1*, page 1, $A + \overline{A}.B = A + B$. Hence, $C + \overline{C}.B = C + B$.
Thus: $\overline{(A.\overline{B}+C)}.\overline{(\overline{A}+B.\overline{C})} = \overline{A}.(B + C)$.

Problem 7 Simplify $\overline{(A.B+\overline{C})}.\overline{(A+.\overline{B}.C)}$

By de Morgan's law (1), $\overline{(A.B+\overline{C})} = \overline{A.B}.\overline{\overline{C}} = \overline{A.B}.C$ by law 18 of *Table 1,* page 1
By de Morgan's law (2), $\overline{A.B} = \overline{A}+\overline{B}$
Hence $\overline{(A.B+\overline{C})} = (\overline{A}+\overline{B}).C = \overline{A}.C + \overline{B}.C$ by law 5
By de Morgan's law (1), $\overline{(A+\overline{B}.C)} = \overline{A}.\overline{\overline{B}.C}$
By de Morgan's law (2), $\overline{\overline{B}.C} = \overline{\overline{B}}+\overline{C} = B+\overline{C}$, by law 18
Hence $\overline{(A+\overline{B}.C)} = \overline{A}.(B+\overline{C}) = \overline{A}.B + \overline{A}.\overline{C}$ by law 5
Thus $\overline{(A.B+\overline{C})}.\overline{(A+\overline{B}.C)} = (\overline{A}.C + \overline{B}.C).(\overline{A}.B + \overline{A}.\overline{C})$
$$= \overline{A}.C.\overline{A}.B + \overline{A}.C.\overline{A}.\overline{C} + \overline{B}.C.\overline{A}.B + \overline{B}.C.\overline{A}.\overline{C} \text{ by law 5}$$
$$= \overline{A}.B.C, \text{ since } \overline{A}.\overline{A} = \overline{A} \text{ from law 13,}$$
$$C.\overline{C} = B.\overline{B} = 0, \text{ from law 14,}$$
and $\overline{A}.0 = 0, \overline{A}.C.0 = 0,$ and $\overline{A}.\overline{B}.0 = 0$ from law 11.

Problem 8 Devise a logic system to meet the requirements of:
$$Z = A.\overline{B} + C.$$

With reference to *Fig 6* and **invert**-gate, shown as (1), gives $\overline{B}$. The **AND**-gate

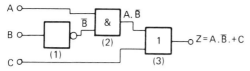

Fig 6

shown as (2), has input of A and $\bar{B}$, giving $A.\bar{B}$. The **OR**-gate, shown as (3), has inputs of $A.\bar{B}$ and C, giving

$Z = A.\bar{B} + C.$

Problem 9 Devise a logic system to meet the requirements of
$(P + \bar{Q}).(\bar{R} + S).$

The logic system is shown in *Fig 7*. The given expression shows that two **invert**-functions are needed to give $\bar{Q}$ and $\bar{R}$ and these are shown as gates (1) and (2).

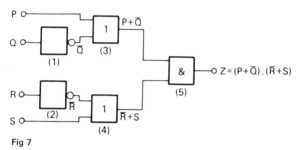

Fig 7

Two **OR**-gates, shown as (3) and (4), give $(P + \bar{Q})$ and $(\bar{R} + S)$ respectively. Finally, an **AND**-gate, shown as (5), gives the required output,

$Z = (P + \bar{Q}).(\bar{R} + S).$

Problem 10 Devise a logic circuit to meet the requirements of the output given in *Table 3*, using as few gates as possible.

Table 3

Inputs			Output
A	B	C	Z
0	0	0	0
0	0	1	0
0	1	0	0
0	1	1	0
1	0	0	0
1	0	1	1
1	1	0	1
1	1	1	1

The "1" outputs in rows 6, 7 and 8 of *Table 3* show that the Boolean expression is:

$$Z = A.\overline{B}.C + A.B.\overline{C} + A.B.C.$$

The logic circuit for this expression can be built using three, 3-input **AND**-gates and one, 3-input **OR**-gate, together with two **invert**-gates. However, the number of gates required can be reduced by using the techniques introduced in chapter 1, resulting in the cost of the circuit being reduced.

Using the laws and rules of Boolean algebra (see *Table 1*, page 1):

$$\begin{aligned}
Z &= A.\overline{B}.C + A.B.\overline{C} + A.B.C \\
&= A.[\overline{B}.C + B.\overline{C} + B.C] \\
&= A.[\overline{B}.C + B.(\overline{C} + C)] \\
&= A.[\overline{B}.C + B] \\
&= A.[B + \overline{B}.C]
\end{aligned}$$

Hence, $\mathbf{Z} = A.(B+C)$

The logic circuit to give this simplified expression is shown in *Fig 8*.

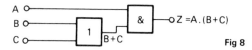

Fig 8

Problem 11 Simplify the expression:

$$Z = \overline{P}.\overline{Q}.R.\overline{S} + \overline{P}.\overline{Q}.R.S + \overline{P}.Q.\overline{R}.\overline{S} + \overline{P}.Q.\overline{R}.S + P.\overline{Q}.R.\overline{S}$$

and devise a logic circuit to give this output.

Applying the rules of Boolean algebra, given in *Table 1*, page 1, gives:

$$Z = \overline{P}.\overline{Q}.R.(\overline{S}+S) + \overline{P}.Q.\overline{R}.(\overline{S}+S) + P.\overline{Q}.R.\overline{S}$$

and since $\overline{S}+S=1$ and $A.1=A$, then

$$\begin{aligned}
Z &= \overline{P}.\overline{Q}.R + \overline{P}.Q.\overline{R} + P.\overline{Q}.R.\overline{S} \\
&= \overline{Q}.\overline{R}.(\overline{P}+P.\overline{S}) + \overline{P}.Q.\overline{R}
\end{aligned}$$

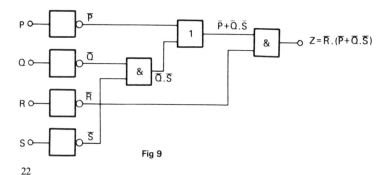

Fig 9

From Rule 17, $A + \overline{A}.B = A + B$, hence
$(\overline{P} + P.\overline{S}) = (\overline{P} + \overline{S})$, i.e.,

$$Z = \overline{Q}.\overline{R}.(\overline{P} + \overline{S}) + \overline{P}.Q.\overline{R}$$
$$= \overline{P}.\overline{Q}.\overline{R} + \overline{Q}.\overline{R}.\overline{S} + \overline{P}.Q.\overline{R}$$
$$= \overline{R}.(\overline{P}.\overline{Q} + \overline{Q}.\overline{S} + \overline{P}.Q)$$
$$= \overline{R}.[\overline{P}.(\overline{Q} + Q) + \overline{Q}.\overline{S}]$$
$$= \overline{R}.(\overline{P} + \overline{Q}.\overline{S})$$

i.e., the simplified expression is $Z = \overline{R}.(\overline{P} + \overline{Q}.\overline{S})$

The logic circuit to produce this expression is shown in *Fig. 9*.

Problem 12 Show how **invert, AND, OR** and **NOR**-functions can be produced using **NAND**-gates only.

A single input to a **NAND**-gate gives the **invert**-function, as shown in *Fig 10(a)*. When two **NAND**-gates are connected, as shown in *Fig 10(b)*, the output from the first gate is $\overline{A.B.C}$ and this is inverted by the second gate, giving

$$Z = \overline{\overline{A.B.C.}} = A.B.C,$$

i.e., the **AND**-function is produced.

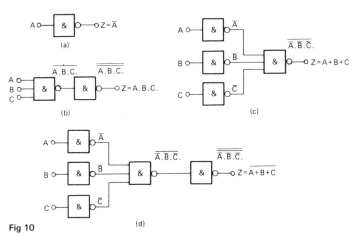

Fig 10

When $\overline{A}$, $\overline{B}$ and $\overline{C}$ are the inputs to a **NAND**-gate, the output is $\overline{\overline{A}.\overline{B}.\overline{C}}$. By de Morgan's law (2),

$$\overline{\overline{A}.\overline{B}.\overline{C}} = \overline{\overline{A}} + \overline{\overline{B}} + \overline{\overline{C}} = A + B + C,$$

i.e. a **NAND**-gate is used to produce the **OR**-function. The logic circuit is shown in *Fig 10(c)*.

If the output from the logic circuit in *Fig 10(c)* is inverted by adding an additional **NAND**-gate, the output becomes the invert of an **OR**-function, i.e. the **NOR**-function, as shown in *Fig 10(d)*.

Problem 13 Design a logic circuit, using **NAND**-gates having not more than three inputs, to meet the requirements of the Boolean equation:

$$Z = \overline{A} + \overline{B} + C + \overline{D}.$$

When designing logic circuits, it is often easier to start at the output of the circuit. The given expression shows there are four variables, joined by **OR**-functions. From the principles introduced in *Problem 12,* if a four-input **NAND**-gate is used to give the required expression, the inputs are $\overline{\overline{A}}$, $\overline{\overline{B}}, \overline{C}$, and $\overline{\overline{D}}$ that is, $A, B, \overline{C}$, and D.

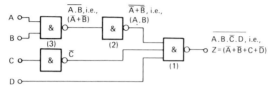

Fig 11

However, the problem states that three-inputs are not to be exceeded, so two of the variables are joined, i.e., the inputs to the three-input **NAND**-gate, shown as gate (1) in *Fig 11,* is $A.B$, $\overline{C}$ and D. From *Problem 12,* the **AND**-function is generated by using two **NAND**-gates connected in series, as shown by gates (2) and (3) in *Fig 11*. The logic circuit required to produce the given equation is as shown in *Fig 11*.

Problem 14 Using **NAND**-gates only devise the logic system representing the Boolean expression $A.B + C$.

Starting at the output of the system $\overline{\overline{A.B} + C} \equiv \overline{\overline{(A.B)}.\overline{C}}$ by applying de Morgan's laws, i.e. (i) $(A.B.)$ is inverted to $\overline{(A.B)}$, C is inverted to $\overline{C}$, (ii) the $+$ is changed to $\cdot$ i.e. $\overline{(A.B)}.\overline{C}$ and (iii) the whole expression is inverted, i.e. $\overline{\overline{(A.B)}.\overline{C}}$ (see para. 2).

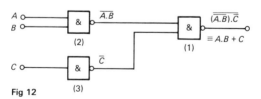

Fig 12

Thus the inputs to **NAND**-gate (1) of *Fig 12* are $(\overline{A.B})$ and $\overline{C}$ and these are produced by **NAND**-gates (2) and (3) respectively. *Fig 12* represent the logic system $A.B + C$ using **NAND**-gates only.

Problem 15 (a) Determine the output Z for the logic circuit shown in *Fig 13*.
(b) Transform the logic circuit shown in *Fig 13* so that universal **NAND**-gates only are used.

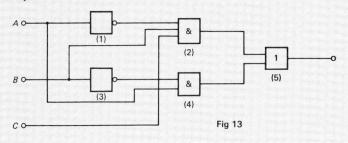

Fig 13

(a) The output of **invert**-gate (1) in *Fig 13* is $\overline{A}$; the output of **AND**-gate (2) is $\overline{A}.B.C$; the output of **invert**-gate (3) is $\overline{B}$; the output of **AND**-gate (4) is $A.\overline{B}$; the output of **OR**-gate (5) is

$$Z = \overline{A}.B.C + A.\overline{B}$$

(b) Applying de Morgan's laws to $\overline{A}.B.C + A.\overline{B}$ gives

$\overline{(\overline{\overline{A}.B.C}).(\overline{A.\overline{B}})}$ — see para. 2.

Thus if the output of a logic circuit is to be

$$\overline{A}.B.C + A.\overline{B}$$

then the inputs to the final **NAND**-gate (shown as (1) in *Fig 14*) are $\overline{\overline{A}.B.C}$ and $\overline{A.\overline{B}}$. If the output of **NAND**-gate (2) is $\overline{\overline{A}.B.C}$ then the inputs are $\overline{A}$ and B and C. The term $\overline{A}$ is produced by **NAND**-gate (3), as shown. If the output of **NAND**-gate (4) is $\overline{A.\overline{B}}$. then the inputs are A and $\overline{B}$. The term $\overline{B}$ is produced by **NAND**-gate (5) as shown.

Fig 14 represents with **NAND**-gates only the logic circuit of *Fig 13*.

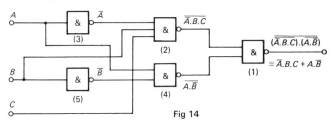

Fig 14

Problem 16 Use **NAND**-gates only to devise the logic system $\overline{P}.Q + \overline{Q}.R$.

By de Morgan's laws

$\overline{P}.Q + \overline{Q}.R \equiv \overline{(\overline{\overline{P}.Q}).(\overline{\overline{Q}.R})}$ — see para. 2.

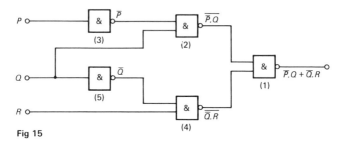

Fig 15

Hence, since the output of the final **NAND**-gate (shown as gate (1) in *Fig 15*). is $\bar{P}.Q + \bar{Q}.R$, then the inputs are $\overline{(\bar{P}.Q)}$ and $\overline{(\bar{Q}.R)}$. Since the output of **NAND**-gate (2) is $\overline{(\bar{P}.Q)}$ then the inputs are $\bar{P}$ and Q, the $\bar{P}$ being produced by **NAND**-gate (3).

Since the output of **NAND**-gate (4) is $\overline{(\bar{Q}.R)}$ then the inputs are $\bar{Q}$ and R, the $\bar{Q}$ being produced by **NAND**-gate (5). The logic network of *Fig 15* represents $\bar{P}.Q + \bar{Q}.R$ using **NAND**-gates only.

Problem 17 Simplify the Boolean expression $A.B.\bar{C} + \bar{A}.\bar{B}.\bar{C} + A.\bar{B}.\bar{C}$. using (a) the laws and rules of Boolean algebra; (b) a Karnaugh map; (c) Devise a logic network to produce the minimised expression using **NAND**-gates only.

(a) With reference to *Table 1*, page 1): *Reference*

$$A.B.\bar{C} + \bar{A}.\bar{B}.\bar{C} + A.\bar{B}.\bar{C} = A.B.\bar{C} + \bar{B}.\bar{C}.(A + \bar{A})$$ 5
$$= A.B.\bar{C} + \bar{B}.\bar{C}. 1$$ 10
$$= A.B.\bar{C} + \bar{B}.\bar{C}$$ 12
$$= \bar{C}.(B + A.B)$$ 5
$$= \bar{C}.(\bar{B} + A)$$ 17

(b) The terms of the expression $A.B.\bar{C} + \bar{A}.\bar{B}.\bar{C} + A.\bar{B}.\bar{C}$ are plotted on the Karnaugh map as shown in *Table 4*, ($A.B.\bar{C}$ being equivalent to 110, and so on). Two couples are formed as shown. Terms common to the couple formed by the two cells on the far right of the top row are A and $\bar{C}$, i.e. $A.\bar{C}$. Terms common to the couple formed by the cells on the far left and far right of the top row are $\bar{B}$ and $\bar{C}$, i.e., $\bar{B}.\bar{C}$. Hence the simplified expression is $A.\bar{C} + \bar{B}.\bar{C}$ which is equivalent to $\bar{C}.(A + \bar{B})$.

Table 4

C \ A.B	00	01	11	10
0	1		1	1
1				

(c) To obtain an output of $\bar{C}.(A + \bar{B})$ from the final **NAND**-gate (shown as (1) in *Fig 16*) an input of $\overline{\bar{C}.(A + \bar{B})}$ is required from **NAND**-gate (2). The inputs to gate (2) are $\bar{C}$ and $(A + \bar{B})$. The term $\bar{C}$ is obtained from gate (3). By de Morgan's laws $(A + \bar{B}) \equiv \overline{\bar{A}.B}$. Thus inputs to gate (4) of $\bar{A}$ and B are necessary, the $\bar{A}$ term being produced by **NAND**-gate (5). *Fig 16* thus represents the system $\bar{C}.(A + \bar{B})$.

26

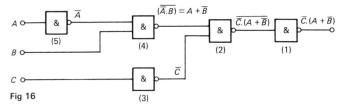

Fig 16

If the minimised expression $A.\overline{C} + \overline{B}.\overline{C}$ is used instead of $\overline{C}.(A + \overline{B})$ then a different logic circuit results. Applying de Morgan's laws to $A.\overline{C} + \overline{B}.\overline{C}$ gives

$\overline{(\overline{A.\overline{C}}).(\overline{\overline{B}.\overline{C}})}$ — see para 2.

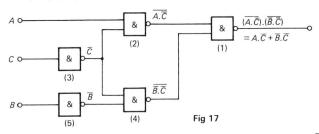

Fig 17

Thus the inputs to the final **NAND**-gate (shown as (1) in *Fig 17*) are $\overline{(A.\overline{C})}$ and $\overline{\overline{B}.\overline{C}}$. For an output of $\overline{(A.\overline{C})}$ from gate (2), inputs of A and $\overline{C}$ are required, the $\overline{C}$ being obtained from gate (3). For an output of $\overline{(\overline{B}.\overline{C})}$ from gate (4), inputs of $\overline{B}$ and $\overline{C}$ are required, these being obtained from gates (5) and (3) respectively. *Fig 17* thus represents the system $A.\overline{C} + \overline{B}.\overline{C}$

Problem 18 Show how **invert, OR, AND** and **NAND**-functions can be produced by using **NOR**-gates only.

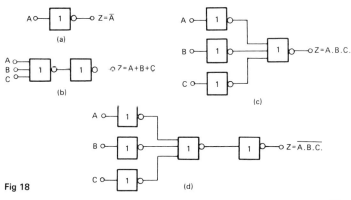

Fig 18

A single input to a **NOR**-gate gives the **invert**-function, as shown in *Fig 18(a)*. When two **NOR**-gates are connected, as shown in *Fig 18(b)*, the output from the first gate is $\overline{A + B + C}$ and this is inverted by the second gate, giving $Z = \overline{\overline{A + B + C}} = A + B + C$, i.e., the **OR**-function is produced. Inputs of $\overline{A}$, $\overline{B}$ and $\overline{C}$ to a **NOR**-gate give an output of $\overline{\overline{A} + \overline{B} + \overline{C}}$. By de Morgan's law: $\overline{\overline{A} + \overline{B} + \overline{C}} = \overline{\overline{A}}.\overline{\overline{B}}.\overline{\overline{C}} = A.B.C$, i.e., the **NOR**-gate can be used to produce the **AND**-function. The logic circuit is shown in *Fig 18(c)*. When the output of the logic circuit, shown in *Fig 18(c)* is inverted by adding an additional **NOR**-gate, the output then becomes the **invert** of an **OR**-function, i.e., the **NOR**-function as shown in *Fig 18(d)*.

Problem 19 Use **NOR**-gates only to design a logic circuit to meet the requirements of the equation:

$$Z = \overline{D}.(\overline{A} + B + \overline{C}).$$

It is usual in logic circuit design to start the design at the output. From *Problem 18*, the **AND**-function between $\overline{D}$ and the terms in the bracket can be produced by using inputs of $\overline{\overline{D}}$ and $\overline{\overline{A} + B + \overline{C}}$ to a **NOR**-gate, i.e., by de Morgan's law, inputs of D and $A.\overline{B}.C$. Again, with reference to *Problem 18*, inputs of $\overline{A}$, B and $\overline{C}$ to a **NOR**-gate give an output of $\overline{\overline{A} + B + \overline{C}}$, which by de Morgan's law is $A.\overline{B}.C$. The logic circuit to produce the required equation is as shown in *Fig 19*.

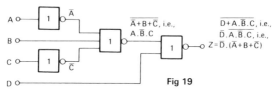

Fig 19

Problem 20 Use **NOR**-gates only to devise the logic system represented by the Boolean expression $(\overline{A} + B).(\overline{C} + \overline{D})$.

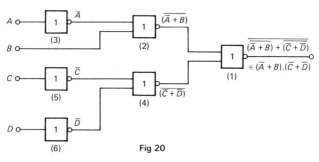

Fig 20

The required logic system is shown in *Fig 20*.
The output of **NOR**-gate (1) is $(\overline{A} + B).(\overline{C} + \overline{D})$ which, by de Morgan's laws, is equivalent to

$\overline{\overline{(\overline{A} + B)} + \overline{(\overline{C} + \overline{D})}}$ — see para. 2.

Thus the inputs to gate (1) are $\overline{(\overline{A} + B)}$ and $\overline{(\overline{C} + \overline{D})}$. An output of $(\overline{A} + B)$ from **NOR**-gate (2) is achieved by inputs of A and B, the $\overline{A}$ term being produced by **NOR**-gate (3). An output of $(\overline{C} + \overline{D})$ from **NOR**-gate (4) is achieved by inputs of $\overline{C}$ and $\overline{D}$, these terms being produced by **NOR**-gates (5) and (6) respectively.

Problem 21 (a) Determine the output Z for the logic network shown in *Fig 21*. (b) Transform the logic network shown in *Fig 21* so that only universal **NOR**-gates are used.

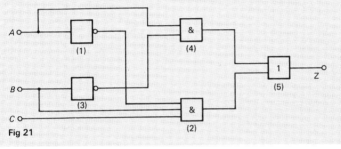

Fig 21

(a) The output of **invert**-gate (1) is $\overline{A}$; the output of **AND**-gate (2) is $\overline{A}.B.C$; the output of **invert**-gate (3) is $\overline{B}$; the output of **AND**-gate (4) is $A.\overline{B}$; the output of **OR**-gate (5) is $Z = \overline{A}.B.C + A.\overline{B}$.

(b) The logic network using **NOR**-gates only is shown in *Fig 22*.
For the output of **NOR**-gate (1) to be $(A.\overline{B} + \overline{A}.B.C)$ the input needs to be $\overline{(A.\overline{B} + \overline{A}.B.C)}$ which is the output of **NOR**-gate (2). The inputs to gate (2) are thus $A.\overline{B}$ and $\overline{A}.B.C$. The output of **NOR**-gate (3), i.e., $A.\overline{B}$ is equivalent to $\overline{\overline{A} + B}$ by de Morgan's laws. Thus the inputs to gate (2) are

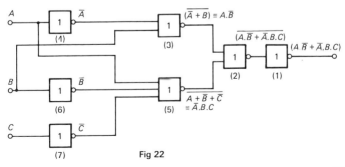

Fig 22

$\bar{A}$ and B, the $\bar{A}$ term being obtained by gate (4). The output of gate (5) is $\overline{\bar{A}.B.C}$ which is equivalent to $A + \bar{B} + \bar{C}$ by de Morgan's laws. Thus the inputs to gate (5) are A, $\bar{B}$ and $\bar{C}$, the $\bar{B}$ and $\bar{C}$ terms being produced by gates (6) and (7) respectively.

Problem 22 Simplify the Boolean expression

$$\bar{P}.\bar{Q}.\bar{R}.S + \bar{P}.Q.R.S + \bar{P}.Q.R.\bar{S} + \bar{P}.Q.\bar{R}S$$

and devise a logic network capable of producing the minimised expression using **NOR**-gates only.

$$\bar{P}.\bar{Q}.\bar{R}.S + \bar{P}.Q.R.S + \bar{P}.Q.R.\bar{S} + \bar{P}.Q.\bar{R}.S = \bar{P}.\bar{R}.S(\bar{Q}+Q) + \bar{P}.Q.R(S+\bar{S})$$
$$= \bar{P}.\bar{R}.S + \bar{P}.Q.R$$
$$= \bar{P}.(Q.R + \bar{R}.S)$$

The logic network representing this minimised expression using **NOR**-gates only is shown in *Fig 23*. The output of **NOR**-gate (1), $\bar{P}.(Q.R + \bar{R}.S)$, is equivalent

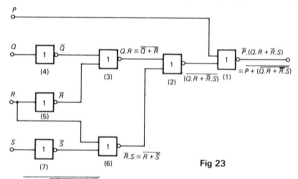

Fig 23

to $\overline{P + (\overline{Q.R} + \overline{\bar{R}.S})}$ by de Morgan's laws. Thus the inputs to gate (1) are P and $\overline{Q.R} + \overline{\bar{R}.S}$. The latter term is the output of gate (2) which means that the inputs to this gate are $Q.R$ and $\bar{R}.S$. The output of gate (3) is $Q.R$, which, by de Morgan's laws is equivalent to $\bar{Q} + \bar{R}$. Thus the inputs to gate (3) are $\bar{Q}$ and $\bar{R}$, which are produced by gates (4) and (5) respectively. The output of gate (6) is $\bar{R}.S$ which, by de Morgan's laws, is equivalent to $R + \bar{S}$. Thus the inputs to gate (6) are R and $\bar{S}$, the latter term being obtained from gate (7).

Problem 23 An alarm indicator in a grinding mill complex should be activated if (a) the power supply to all mills is off and (b) the hopper feeding the mills is less than 10% full, and (c) if less than two of the three grinding mills are in action. Devise a logic system to meet these requirements.

Let variable A represent the power supply on to all the mills, then $\bar{A}$ represents the power supply off. Let B represent the hopper feeding the mills being more than 10% full, then $\bar{B}$ represents the hopper being less than 10% full. Let C, D and E represent the three mills respectively being in action, then $\bar{C}$, $\bar{D}$ and $\bar{E}$ represent the three mills respectively not being in action. The required equation to activate the alarm is:

$$Z = \bar{A}.\bar{B}.(\bar{C} + \bar{D} + \bar{E}).$$

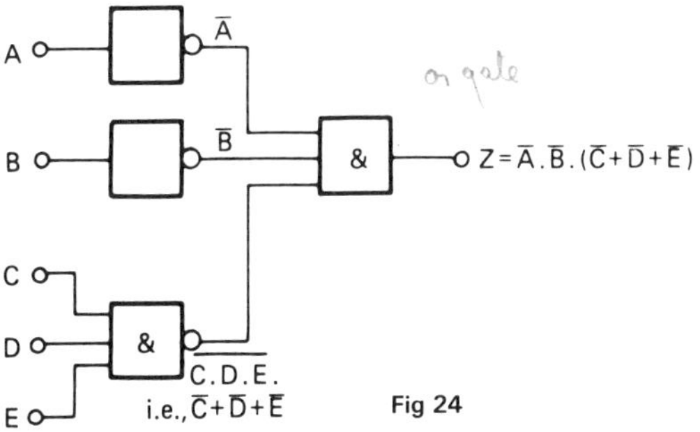

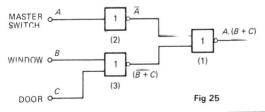

Fig 24

There are three variables joined by **AND**-functions in the output, indicating that a three-input **AND**-gate is required, having inputs of $\bar{A}$, $\bar{B}$ and $(\bar{C} + \bar{D} + \bar{E})$. The term $(\bar{C} + \bar{D} + \bar{E})$ is produced by a three-input **NAND**-gate. When variables C, D and E are the inputs to a **NAND**-gate, the output is $\overline{C.D.E}$, which, by de Morgan's law is $\bar{C} + \bar{D} + \bar{E}$. Hence the required logic circuit is as shown in *Fig 24*.

Problem 24 A burglar alarm system has a master switch A to switch the system on, a switch B on the window and a switch C on the door. Devise a logic network using universal nor-gates to ring the bell when the master switch is on and when either the window or the door switches are on.

The Boolean expression for the given conditions is A and $(B$ or $C)$, i.e., $A.(B + C)$. The logic network using **NOR**-gates only is shown in *Fig 25*.

Fig 25

The output of gate (1), $A.(B + C)$ is equivalent $\overline{\bar{A} + \overline{(B + C)}}$, by de Morgan's laws. Hence the inputs to gate (1) are $\bar{A}$ and $\overline{(B + C)}$. Gate (2) produces $\bar{A}$ and gate (3) produces $\overline{(B + C)}$ as shown.

Problem 25 A dust-free area has two entrances each having two doors as shown in *Fig 26*. A warning bell must sound if both doors A and B or doors C and D are open at the same time. State the Boolean expression depicting this occurrence and devise a logic network to operate the bell using (a) **NAND**-gates only, and (b) **NOR**-gates only.

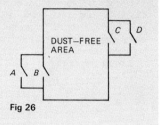

Fig 26

The Boolean expression depicting the occurrence of both doors A and B or doors C and D open at the same time is: $A.B + C.D$.

(a) A logic network using **NAND**-gates only is shown in *Fig 27*. The output of gate (1), $A.B + C.D$ is equivalent to $\overline{(\overline{A.B}).(\overline{C.D})}$ by de Morgan's laws.

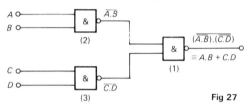

Fig 27

Hence the inputs to gate (1) are $(\overline{A.B})$ and $(\overline{C.D})$. The output of gate (2), $(\overline{A.B})$ is obtained by inputs of A and B. The outputs of gate (3), $(\overline{C.D})$ is obtained by inputs of C and D as shown.

(b) A logic network using **NOR**-gates only is shown in *Fig 28*. The output of gate (1) is $A.B + C.D$ and hence the input to gate (1) is $\overline{A.B. + C.D}$. Since the output of gate (2) is $\overline{A.B. + C.D}$ then the inputs to gate (2) are $A.B$ and $C.D$. The output of gate (3), $A.B$ is equivalent to $\overline{\overline{A} + \overline{B}}$ by de Morgan's laws, the terms $\overline{A}$ and $\overline{B}$ being generated by gates (4) and (5) respectively. The output of gate (6), $C.D$ is equivalent to $\overline{(\overline{C} + \overline{D})}$ by de Morgan's laws, the terms $\overline{C}$ and $\overline{D}$ being generated by gates (7) and (8) respectively. It is noted that in this case a far simpler logic network is produced using **NAND**-gates than using **NOR**-gates.

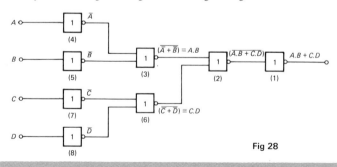

Fig 28

C FURTHER PROBLEMS ON LOGIC CIRCUITS

In Problems 1 to 10, use de Morgan's laws and the rules of Boolean algebra given in Table 1, page 1, to minimise the given expressions.

1. $\overline{(\overline{A.B})}$ $[A + \overline{B}]$

2. $\overline{(\overline{\overline{P} + Q})}$ $[P.Q]$

3. $(\overline{A}.\overline{B}).(\overline{\overline{A}.B})$ $[\overline{A}.\overline{B}]$

4. $\overline{\overline{A} + \overline{B}} + \overline{B}$ $[\overline{B}]$

5. $\overline{(A + \overline{B.\overline{C}})} + \overline{(A.\overline{B} + C)}$ $[\overline{A} + \overline{B} + C]$

6. $(\overline{\overline{A} + A.B}).(\overline{A} + A.B)$ $[A.\overline{B}]$

7. $(\overline{\overline{A}.B + B.\overline{C}}).(\overline{A.\overline{B}})$ $[\overline{A}.\overline{B} + A.B.C]$

8. $(\overline{\overline{P.Q.R}}).(\overline{P + Q.\overline{R}})$ $[\overline{P}.\overline{Q}]$

9. $(A.\overline{B} + B.\overline{C}) + (\overline{A}.B)$ $[1]$

10. $(P.\overline{Q} + \overline{P}.R).\overline{P.Q.R}$ $[\overline{P}.(Q + \overline{R})]$

In Problems 11 to 15, devise logic systems to meet the requirements of the Boolean equations given.

11. $Z = \overline{A} + B.C$ [See *Fig 29(a)*]

12. $Z = A.\overline{B} + B.\overline{C}$ [See *Fig 29(b)*]

13. $Z = A.B.\overline{C} + \overline{A}.\overline{B}.C$ [See *Fig 29(c)*]

14. $Z = (\overline{A} + B).(\overline{C} + D)$ [See *Fig 29(d)*]

15. $Z = A.\overline{B} + B.\overline{C} + C.\overline{D}$ [See *Fig 29(e)*]

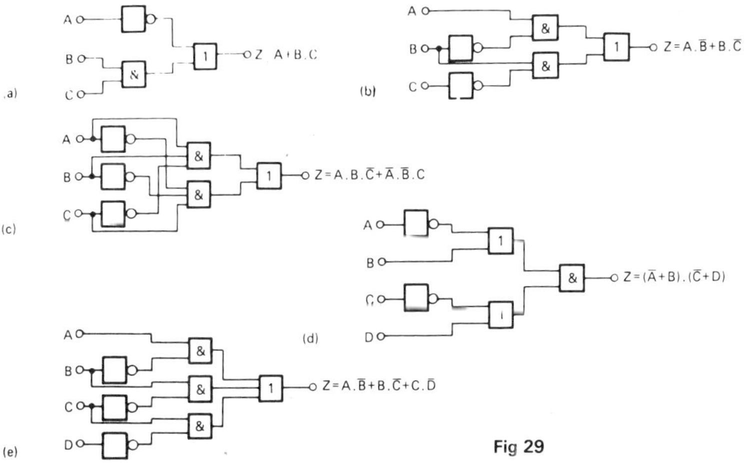

Fig 29

In Problems 16 to 18 simplify the expression given in the truth table and devise a logic circuit to meet the requirements stated.

16 Column 4 of *Table 5*   [$A.B+C$, see *Fig 30(a)*]

17 Column 5 of *Table 5*   [$A.\overline{B}+B.C$, see *Fig 30(b)*]

18 Column 6 of *Table 5*   [$A.C+B$, see *Fig 30(c)*]

Table 5

1 A	2 B	3 C	4 Z_1	5 Z_2	6 Z_3
0	0	0	0	0	0
0	0	1	1	0	0
0	1	0	0	0	1
0	1	1	1	1	1
1	0	0	0	1	0
1	0	1	1	1	1
1	1	0	1	0	1
1	1	1	1	1	1

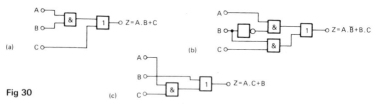

Fig 30

In Problems 19 to 25, simplify the Boolean expression given and devise logic circuits to give the requirements of the simplified expressions.

19 $\overline{P}.\overline{Q}+\overline{P}.Q+P.Q$ [$\overline{P}+Q$, see *Fig 31(a)*]

20 $\overline{P}.\overline{Q}.\overline{R}.+P.Q.\overline{R}+P.\overline{Q}.\overline{R}$ [$\overline{R}.(P+\overline{Q})$, see *Fig 31(b)*]

21 $P.\overline{Q}.R+P.\overline{Q}.\overline{R}+\overline{P}.\overline{Q}.\overline{R}$ [$\overline{Q}.(P+\overline{R})$, see *Fig 31(c)*]

22 $\overline{P}.\overline{Q}.R+P.Q.\overline{R}+P.Q.R+P.\overline{Q}.R$ [$\overline{P}.\overline{Q}.R+P.(.Q+R)$, see *Fig 31(d)*]

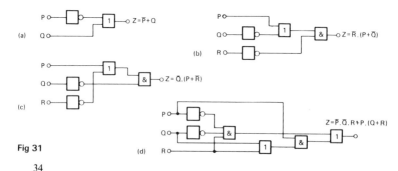

Fig 31

23 $\overline{A}.\overline{B}.\overline{C}.\overline{D}+A.\overline{B}.\overline{C}.\overline{D}+\overline{A}.\overline{B}.C.\overline{D}+\overline{A}.B.C.\overline{D}+A.\overline{B}.C.\overline{D}$
    $[\overline{D}.(\overline{A}.C+\overline{B}),$ see *Fig. 32(a)*]

24 $\overline{A}.\overline{B}.C.\overline{D}+\overline{A}.B.\overline{C}.D+A.B.\overline{C}.D+\overline{A}.B.C.D+A.B.C.D$
    $[\overline{A}.\overline{B}.C.\overline{D}+B.D,$ see *Fig 32(b)*]

25 $(\overline{\overline{P.Q.R}}).(\overline{P+Q.R})$ $[\overline{P}.(\overline{Q}+\overline{R}),$ see *Fig 32(c)*]

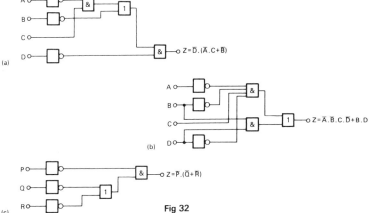

Fig 32

In Problems 26 to 28, use NAND-gates only to devise the logic systems stated.

26 $Z=A+B.C$ [See *Fig 33(a)*]
27 $Z=A.\overline{B}+B.\overline{C}$ [See *Fig 33(b)*]
28 $Z=A.B.\overline{C}+\overline{A}.\overline{B}.C$ [See *Fig 33(c)*]

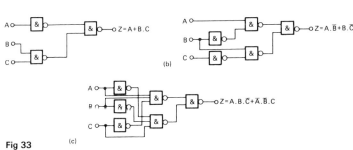

Fig 33

29. Transform the logic network shown in *Fig 32(c)* so that **NAND**-gates only are used. [See *Fig 34*]

35

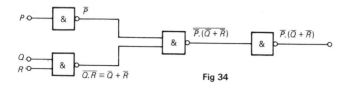

Fig 34

In Problems 30 to 32, use **NOR**-gates only to devise the logic systems stated.

30 $Z = (\bar{A} + B).(\bar{C} + D)$ [See *Fig 35(a)*]

31 $Z = A.\bar{B} + B.\bar{C} + C.\bar{D}$ [See *Fig 35(b)*]

32 $Z = \bar{P}.Q + P.(Q + R)$ [See *Fig 35(c)*]

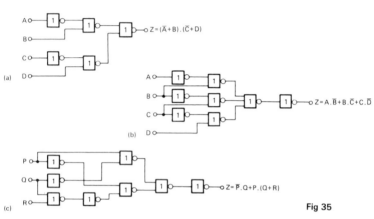

Fig 35

33 Transform the logic network shown in *Fig 32(c)* so that **NOR**-gates only are used. [See *Fig 36*]

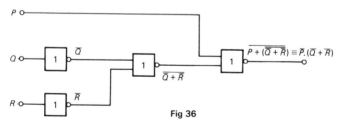

Fig 36

34 (a) State the Boolean expression representing the output Z of the logic network shown in *Fig 37*.
   (b) Redesign the logic network of *Fig 37* so that (i) **NAND**-gates only are used, (ii) **NOR**-gates only are used.

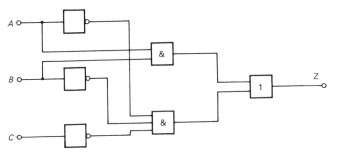

Fig 37

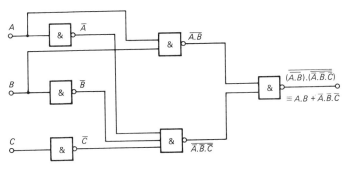

Fig 38

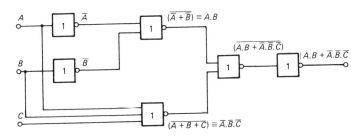

Fig 39

$$\begin{bmatrix} \text{(a)} & Z = A.B + \overline{A}.\overline{B}.\overline{C} \\ \text{(b)} & \text{(i)} \quad \text{See } \textit{Fig 38} \\ & \text{(ii)} \quad \text{See } \textit{Fig 39} \end{bmatrix}$$

35 In a chemical process, three of the transducers used are P, Q and R, giving output signals of either 0 or 1. Devise a logic system to give a 1 output when:
   (a) P and Q and R all have 0 outputs, or when:
   (b) P is 0 and (Q is 1 or R is 0).

$[\overline{P}.(Q + R), \text{ see } \textit{Fig 40(a)}]$

36 Lift doors should close if:
   (a) the master switch, (A), is on and either
   (b) a call, (B) is received from any other floor, or
   (c) the doors, (C) have been open for more than 10 s, or
   (d) the selector push within the lift (D), is pressed for another floor. Devise a logic circuit to meet these requirements.

   [$Z = A.(B + C + D)$, see *Fig 40(b)*]

37 A water tank feeds three separate processes. When any two of the processes are in operation at the same time, a signal is required to start a pump to maintain the head of water in the tank. Devise a logic circuit using **NOR**-gates only to give the required signal.

   [$Z = A.(B + C) + B.C$, see *Fig 40(c)*]

38 A logic signal is required to give an indication when:
   (a) the supply to an oven is on, and
   (b) the temperature of the oven exceeds 210°C, or
   (c) the temperature of the oven is less than 190°C.

   Devise a logic circuit using **NAND**-gates only to meet these requirements.

   [$Z = A.(B + C)$, see *Fig 40(d)*]

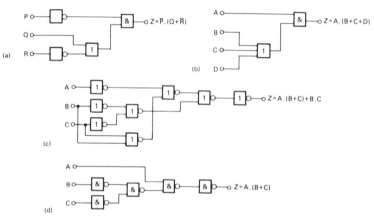

Fig 40

3 Logic families

A. MAIN POINTS CONCERNED WITH LOGIC FAMILIES

1 Many different electronic circuit configurations are available for the construction of logic circuits. A complete set of logic functions which use a common circuit configuration is known as a *'logic family'*. Many different logic families are available in integrated form, and those most commonly used are:

(a) *transistor-transistor logic (TTL)*,
(b) *complementary metal oxide semiconductor (CMOS)*, and
(c) *emitter-coupled logic (ECL)*.

Logic families may be of the saturating or non-saturating type, and selection of a particular family depends upon the application being considered.

2 The most widely used type of saturating logic is *'transistor-transistor logic'* (TTL), which uses special multi-emitter transistors for its fabrication. A wide range of circuit functions from simple gates to complex counters and registers are available in the TTL family. The circuit of a basic positive NAND gate is shown in *Fig 1*.

This circuit operates in the following manner:

(i) *A or B (or both) at logical 0.*

When one (or both) of the input terminals A or B is held at logical 0 (0 V — 0.4 V), TR1 base-emitter junction becomes forward biassed, and base

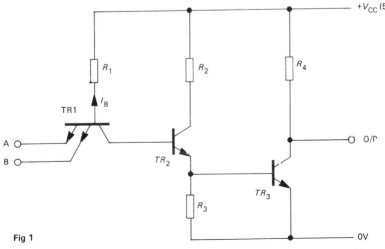

Fig 1

current I_B flows. As a result, TR1 becomes saturated and its collector potential falls to almost 0 V. Therefore TR2 is cut off since it receives insufficient base bias, and this in turn, causes TR3 to be cut off. The collector potential of TR3 rise towards $+V$cc (5 V) and the gate output is therefore at logical 1.

(ii) *A and B both at logical 1*

When both input terminals *A* and *B* are held at logical 1 (2.4 V – 5 V), TR1 base potential rises towards $+V_{CC}$. As a result, the base-collector junction of TR1 becomes forward biassed, and base current I_B is diverted into TR2 base-emitter circuit, thus turning TR2 on. This, in turn, causes TR3 to conduct heavily and its collector potential falls to almost 0 V. The gate output is therefore at logical 0. (*See Problems 1 to 10, 14, 15, and 20.*)

3 Where low power consumption and compact assemblies are required, e.g. battery-operated portable equipment, a very wide range of circuits are available which use *'complementary metal oxide semiconductor'* (CMOS) construction. CMOS circuits are constructed from 'field effect transistors' (FETs), using a mixture of *n*-channel and *p*-channel devices. A typical CMOS NAND gate circuit is shown in *Fig 2*.

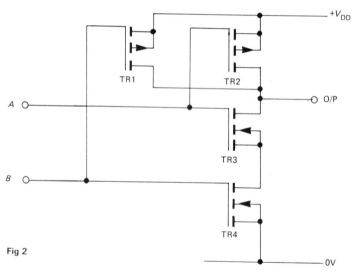

Fig 2

This circuit operates in the following manner:

(i) *A or B (or both) at logical 0.*

When one (or both) of the input terminals *A* or *B* is held at logical 0 (0 V), TR1 or TR2 (or both) are biassed into conduction since they are both *n*-channel devices. TR3 or TR4 (or both), however, are in the non-conducting state with this input, since they are both *p*-channel devices. Therefore, the output potential rises to $+V_{DD}$ and the gate output is at logical 1, as illustrated by the equivalent switching diagram in *Fig. 3(a)*.

(ii) *A and B both at logical 1.*

When both input terminals *A* and *B* are held at logical 1 (3 V – 15 V), TR1 and TR2 are biassed into the non-conducting state since they are both *n*-channel

40

devices. TR3 and TR4, however, are biassed into conduction with this input, since they are both *p*-channel devices. Therefore, the output potential falls to 0 V and the gate output is at logical 0, as illustrated by the equivalent switching diagram, *Fig. 3(b)*. (See Problems 11 to 16 and 20.)

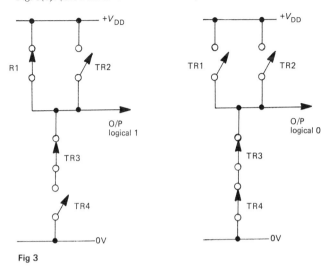

Fig 3

4 For applications that require very fast switching speeds (> 200 MHz), a non-saturating type of logic, known as *'emitter-coupled logic'* (ECL) may be used. The basic circuit for this type of logic consists of two transistors with their emitter circuits coupled — (hence the term 'emitter coupled logic'), and a circuit of this type is shown in *Fig 4*.

The operation of this circuit may be studied by considering TR1 and TR2 operating under the following conditions:

(i) TR1 and TR2 conducting equally,

$$I_1 = I_2 = \tfrac{1}{2} I_s \text{ and } V_1 = V_2$$

(ii) TR1 conducting very much more than TR2

$$I_1 \approx I_s, \quad I_2 \approx 0,$$
and $$V_1 \approx -(I_s \times R_1), \quad V_2 \approx 0$$

(iii) TR1 conducting very much less than TR2

$$I_1 \sim 0, \quad I_2 \approx I_s$$
and $$V_1 \approx 0, \quad V_2 \approx -(I_s \times R_L)$$

Thus, current I_S is switched between TR1 and TR2 according to the conduction of TR1 relative to TR2, and for this reason, ECL is often known as *'current mode logic'* (CML).

Note, for positive logic, 0 V corresponds to logical 1 and $-(I_S \times R_L)$ V corresponds to logical 0.

The circuit of a basic OR/NOR gate using ECL technology is shown in *Fig 5*.

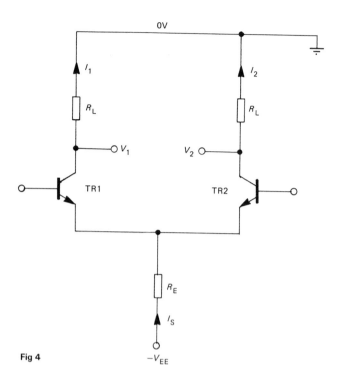

Fig 4

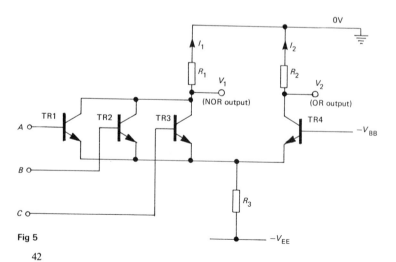

Fig 5

42

This circuit operates in the following manner:

(i) *One or more inputs A, B or C at logical 1.*

When one of the input terminals *A, B* or *C* is held at logical 1 (−0.75 V), TR1, TR2 or TR3 conduct and current I_1 increases, causing an increase in p.d. across R_3. Due to the emitter coupling, TR4 emitter potential rises towards its fixed base potential ($-V_{BB}$) and causes this transistor to cut off, with the result that I_2 falls to zero. Therefore, V_1 falls to logical 0 ($-(V_{BB}+0.6\,\text{V})$) and V_2 rises to logical 1 (0 V).

(ii) *All inputs A, B and C at logical 0.*

When all input terminals *A, B* and *C* are held at logical 0 (−1.55 V), TR1, TR2 and TR3 are all in a non-conducting state, and I_1 falls to zero, causing the p.d. across R_3 to fall also. Due to the emitter coupling, TR4 emitter potential falls relative to its fixed base potential ($-V_{BB}$) and causes this transistor to conduct more heavily. Therefore, I_2 increases and all of the current is diverted through TR4 with the result that V_2 falls to logical 0 ($-(V_{BB}+0.6\,\text{V})$) and V_1 rises to logical 1 (0 V).

From this description, it can be seen that V_1 acts logically as the result of NORing inputs *A, B* and *C*, and V_2 acts logically as the result of ORing inputs, *A, B* and *C*. *(See Problems 17 to 20.)*

B. WORKED PROBLEMS ON LOGIC FAMILIES

Problem 1 Draw the circuit diagram of a dual input TTL NAND-gate.

A typical dual input TTL NAND-gate is the type 7400, and its circuit diagram is shown in *Fig 6* (page 44).

Problem 2 Explain the reason for using an *active load* in a TTL gate output circuit.

One of the factors which limit the switching speed of a gate is capacitance across its output. This capacitance (formed by junction capacitance of the transistors in the gate circuit and stray wiring capacitance) increases greatly as the number of gate inputs connected to an output is increased.

The circuit of a gate output stage which uses a passive load is shown in *Fig 7*. The total circuit capacitances are considered to be lumped together across T_R outputs and depicted as C_S in *Fig 7*.

When a low-to-high transition occurs at the output of this circuit, the output potential is prevented from changing instantaneously, since C_S must first be charged through R_L.

On a high-to-low transition, however, this problem does not occur, since TR is saturated and its low resistance is able to discharge C_S rapidly.

One possible solution to speed up the low-to-high transition is to reduce the value of R_L and thus reduce the charging time for C_S. This greatly increases the power dissipation in the circuit when TR1 is saturated, which is undesirable.

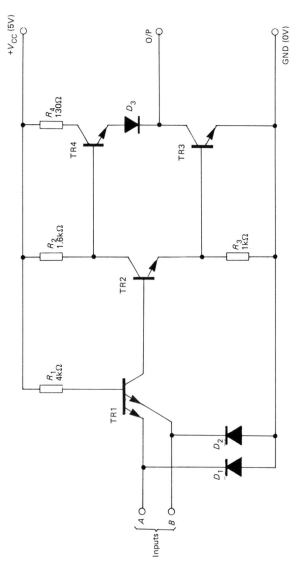

Fig 6

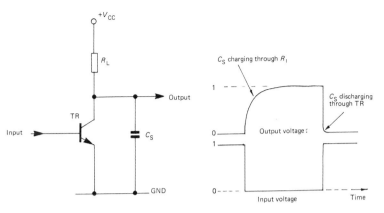

Fig 7

The ideal solution is to have a variable value for R_L, such that it has a high resistance for high-to-low output transitions (TR1 saturated), but a low resistance for low-to-high output transitions (TR1 cut off). Such a solution may be implemented by replacing R_L with a transistor, known as an *'active load'*, and vary its conduction according to circuit requirements. A circuit of this type is shown in *Fig 8*, and is frequently called a *'totem pole'* output stage.

The circuit is arranged such that when TR1 conducts for a high-to-low transition, TR2 is non-conducting (high resistance), (*Fig 8(a)*), and when TR1 is

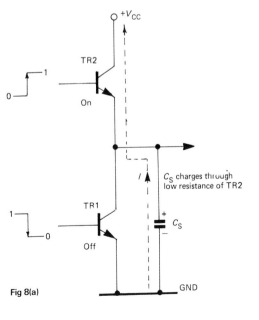

Fig 8(a)

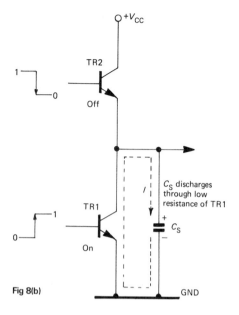

Fig 8(b)

cut off for a low-to-high transition, TR2 is saturated (low resistance) so that C_S is rapidly discharged *(Fig 8(b))*. Driving signals V_1 and V_2 must be at opposite logic levels at any instant in time to achieve correct operation.

Problem 3 A practical 'totem pole' output stage of a TTL gate is shown in *Fig 6*. Explain the function of: (a) R_4, and (b) D_3.

(a) Due to charge storage effects, it takes longer for a transistor to switch from saturation to cut off than it does to switch from cut off to saturation. Therefore, when there is a change in logic state at the gate output, both transistors TR3 and TR4 simultaneously saturate for a short period of time. The function of R_4 is to limit the supply current during the period when both TR3 and TR4 are staturated to prevent excessive disturbance of the supply voltage V_{CC}.
(b) When the gate output is at logical 0, TR2 and TR3 are saturated (ON) and TR4 is cut off (OFF). These conditions are illustrated in *Fig 9*.

From *Fig 9* it can be seen that:

(i)   TR4 base = TR2 collector = $V_{CE_{SAT}} + V_{BE_{SAT}}$
            potential   potential
                                         = 0.3 V + 0.7 V = **1.0 V**,

and   (ii)   if D_3 is considered to be out of circuit,

        TR4 emitter = TR3 collector = $V_{CE_{SAT}}$ = **0.3 V**.
         potential   potential

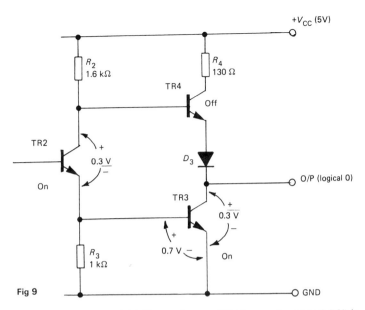

Fig 9

Therefore the potential difference between TR4 base and emitter (0.7 V) is sufficient to cause it to conduct. This is unacceptable, since TR3 is also conducting and a low resistance path across the supply results.

If D_3 is included in series with TR4 emitter, an additional 0.6 V is required on TR4 base to cause conduction, i.e. 1.6 V total. Since TR2 collector potential is only 1.0 V, this is insufficient to cause TR4 to conduct.

When the gate output is at logical 1, D_3 has little effect since the gate output is required to source only a very small current (≈ 40 μA).

Problem 4 Draw the circuit diagram of a quadruple input TTL NAND gate with open collector output.

A typical quadruple TTL NAND gate with open collector output is the type 74LS22, and the circuit diagram of this gate is shown in *Fig 10* (page 48).

Problem 5 Explain the reason for using logic gates with open collector outputs

On occasions it may be necessary to connect the outputs of two (or more) TTL gates in parallel. Two ordinary TTL outputs must not be connected in parallel, since they may try to force each other to opposite logic levels and consequently cause damage. This situation is illustrated in *Fig 11*.

Logic gates *A* and *B* have their outputs connected in parallel. If the input

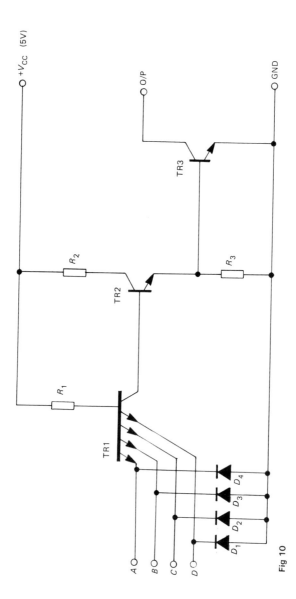

Fig 10

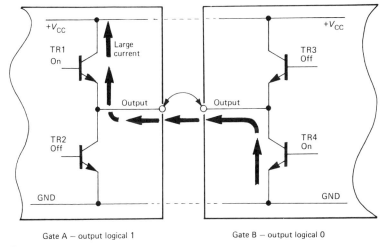

Gate A — output logical 1 Gate B — output logical 0

Fig 11

conditions on gate *A* are such as to cause its output to become logical 1, TR1 is saturated and TR2 is cut off. If the input conditions on gate *B* cause its output to become logical 0, TR3 is cut off and TR4 is saturated. When these conditions occur simultaneously, an excessively large current flows through TR1 and TR4 and this may lead to damage in either or both gates.

Open collector gates are available in which the load resistor of the output stage is missing and must be provided external to the gate IC by its user. The outputs of these gates may be connected in parallel and supplied by a common load resistor (*R*) (see *Fig 12*).

With this configuration, the output is at logical 0 if any one of the outputs of G_1, G_2 or G_3 is at logical 0 level. This arrangement is frequently known as **'wired-OR'** output, although this term is somewhat misleading, since logically this does not give the same result as connecting G_1, G_2 and G_3 outputs to a conventional OR gate.

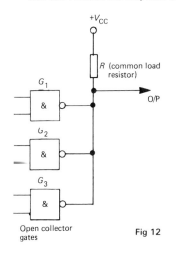

Open collector gates

Fig 12

Problem 6 Describe how the logic levels used in practical TTL circuits are derived.

TTL circuits operate with a supply potential (V_{CC}) of +5 V, and for this reason it is often assumed that the logic levels used are +5 V for logical 1 and 0 V for logical 0.

This may well be the case for externally derived signals, but when considering interconnected TTL circuits a different situation exists. Logic levels are defined as bands of voltage levels rather than fixed values, and the reason for this is that it is not practicable to be precise because of supply variations and circuit loading effects.

When a TTL output is used to source an external load (see *Fig 13(a)*), the logic 1 output voltage level (V_{OH}) may be expressed as:

(i) $V_{OH} = V_{CC} - (I_B \times R_2) - V_{BE} - V_{D3}$

Under most conditions the term $I_B \times R_2$ is very small and may be ignored. Terms V_{BE} and V_{D3} represent volt drops across two forward biassed diodes in the output structure, therefore equation (i) may be simplified to:

(ii) $V_{OH} = V_{CC} - 2 V_{BE}$

The value of V_{BE} used depends upon the output load current value (I_L) and the ambient temperature. Typical values for V_{BE} are quoted in *Table 1*.

When a TTL output is used to sink current from an external load, the logic 0 output voltage level (V_{OL}) may be expressed as:

$V_{OL} = V_{CE_{SAT}}$ (see *Fig 13(b)*)

The value of $V_{CE_{SAT}}$ varies from 0.2 V (small load current) to 0.4 V (max. load current of 16 mA). The voltage levels required at a gate input for a particular logic output level may be determined by reference to the TTL NAND gate circuit shown in *Fig 6*.

To obtain an output of logical 0 from this gate, TR2 and TR3 must be saturated, and TR1 must be cut off with its collector/base junction forward biased. A minimum input potential of 2.4 V is required on both inputs *A* and *B* to maintain this condition.

To obtain an output of logical 1, TR2 and TR3 must be cut off and TR1 must be saturated. A maximum input potential of 0.8 V is required on either input *A* or *B* to maintain this condition.

Table 1

Load current	V_{BE} at 0 °C	V_{BE} at 25 °C
10^{-2} mA	450 mV	500 mV
10^{-1} mA	500 mV	550 mV
1 mA	550 mV	600 mV
10 mA	620 mV	670 mV
100 mA	720 mV	770 mV

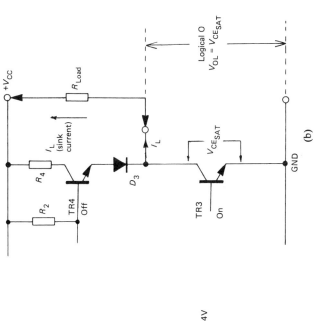

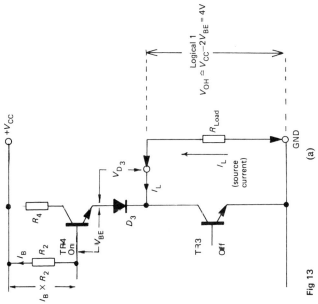

Fig 13

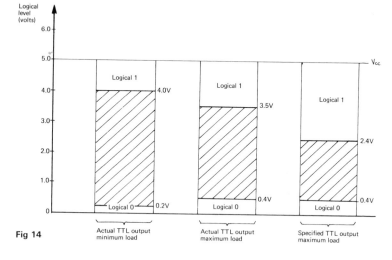

Fig 14

A safety margin of 0.4 V is adopted, so that the maximum logical 0 level at a gate output is specified as 0.4 V less than the maximum logical 0 level permitted at a gate input. Similarly, the minimum logical 1 level at a gate output is specified as 0.4 V more than the minimum logical 1 level permitted at a gate input. These levels are illustrated in *Fig 14*.

Problem 7 With regard to TTL gate circuits, explain: (i) why unused inputs must not be left 'floating', and (ii) how unused inputs may be dealt with in practical logic circuits.

(i) Current pulses due to switching in one part of a logic circuit may cause voltages to be induced in other parts of the circuit. Such induced voltages are known as **'noise'**, and any noise pulse of sufficient amplitude may cause an unwanted change in logic level if it is allowed to reach the input of a logic circuit. This may cause circuit malfunction.

An unconnected or 'floating' TTL input has a potential of approximately 1.6 V, and although this normally acts as a logical 1, it is an undefined level (see *Fig 14*) and is therefore not consistently predictable. Small changes in input voltage may cause a logical input in the undefined region to swing to either logical 0 or logical 1. Therefore, unconnected TTL inputs are more likely to be affected by noise pulses than those inputs which are connected to well defined logic levels.

The amplitude of a noise pulse necessary to cause a logical 0 or a logical 1 input to be driven into the undefined region is known as the circuit **'noise margin'**, and this is typically 400 mV (0.4 V) for TTL circuits. Unused TTL inputs should therefore not be left unconnected if noise problems are to be avoided.

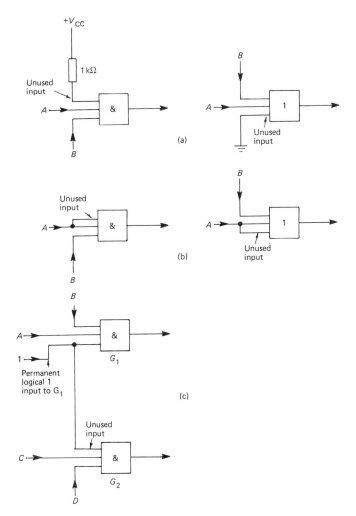

Fig 15

(ii) An unused TTL input may be dealt with in one of the following ways:
(a) connect it to a valid logical 0 or logical 1 level, as appropriate, so that normal circuit operation with the used inputs is maintained (see *Fig 15(a)*),
(b) connect it in parallel with a driven input, provided the fan out of the driving gate is not exceeded (see *Fig 15(b)*), or
(c) connect it to another input (or output) which is permanently held at the appropriate logic level (see *Fig 15(c)*).

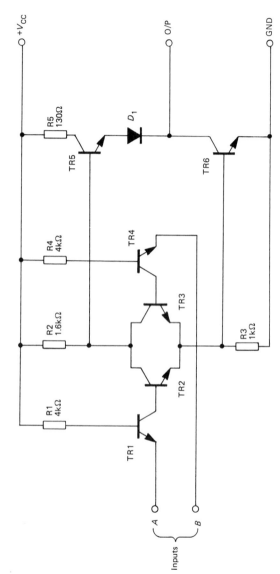

Fig 16

Problem 8 Draw the circuit diagram of a TTL NOR gate and briefly explain its operation.

A typical dual input TTL NOR gate is the type 7402, and its circuit diagram is shown in *Fig 16*.
This circuit operates in the following manner:
(a) **inputs *A* and *B* both at logical 0.**
TR1 and TR4 are both saturated and their collector potentials fall to almost 0 V. This causes TR2 and TR3 to both be cut off and their collector potential rises to $+V_{CC}$ thus biassing TR5 into conduction. TR2/TR3 emitter potential falls to 0 V, thus causing TR6 to be cut off. Therefore the gate output potential rises towards $+V_{CC}$, i.e. logical 1.
(b) **input *A* or input *B* (or both) at logical 1.**
The base/collector junction of either TR1 or TR4 (or both) becomes forward biased, and a large base current flows in either TR2 or TR3 (or both). Therefore TR2 or TR3 (or both) conduct heavily and TR2/3 emitter potential rises, biassing TR6 into conduction. TR2/3 collector potential falls, and this biases TR5 to cut off. Therefore the gate output potential falls towards 0 V, i.e. logical 0.

Problem 9 Explain the meanings of the terms **'unit load'** and **'fan out'** in relation to TTL circuits.

The load imposed by a single, standard TTL input on the output of a circuit to which it is connected is known as a **'unit load' (UL)**. For a standard TTL input, this represents a load current of 1.6 mA at a logical 0 level of 400 mV. The load imposed by other circuits may be expressed in terms of unit loads.

The **'fan out'** of a TTL circuit refers to the number of TTL gate inputs that may be connected to a single TTL output. A TTL output transistor is required to sink a current of 1.6 mA for each standard TTL input connected to it when in the logical 0 state (see *Fig 17*). An increase in the current through this output transistor causes a rise in V_{CESAT}, therefore there is a limit to the number of inputs that may be connected to a TTL output, otherwise the logical 0 level may increase to a value which puts it into the undefined region.

For a standard TTL circuit, the maximum number of unit loads that may safely be connected to a single TTL output is 10, therefore this type of circuit has a fan out of 10. The fan out of open collector TTL circuits is usually 30. The loads imposed by various inputs are shown in *Fig 18*.

Problem 10 Briefly explain the main differences between the following types of TTL devices: (i) 74XX; (ii) 74HXX; (iii) 74LXX; (iv) 74SXX; (v) 74LSXX.

In an ideal logic family, the switching speeds should be as high as possible, and the power consumption as low as possible.

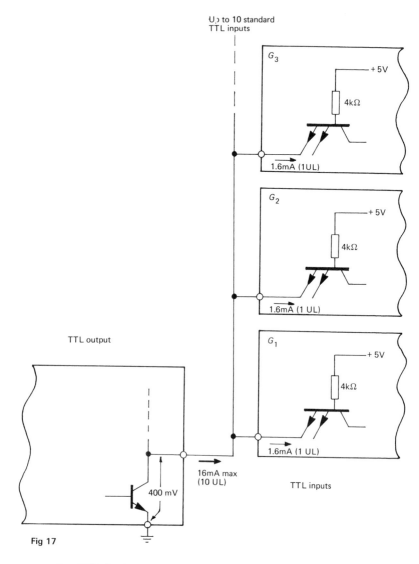

Fig 17

In a TTL circuit, use is made of the various resistors in the circuit to charge and discharge various transistor and stray capacitances, and the time constants so formed ($C \times R$) determine the maximum switching speed. Also, since one or more transistors are conducting at any given time in a TTL circuit, current paths are provided through the circuit resistors which keeps the power consumption of such circuits high.

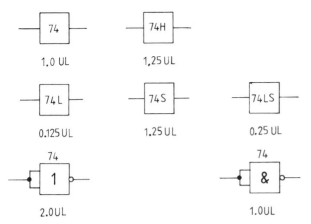

Fig 18

The various TTL families available offer variations on the conflicting requirements of low power consumption and fast switching times.

(i) **74XX series**   This is the **'standard' TTL** family, and represents a compromise between low power consumption and high switching speed. Typical power consumption is 10 mW per gate and switching time is 10 ns.

(ii) **74HXX series**   This is a **high speed TTL** family, and the faster switching speed is obtained by using lower resistance values throughout to shorten the internal CR time constants. This inevitably results in higher power consumption. Typical power consumption is 22 mW per gate and a switching time of 6 ns.

(iii) **74LXX series**   This is a **lower power consumption TTL** family. The reduction in power consumption is obtained by increasing the resistor values throughout. This inevitably results in slower switching speeds, since the internal CR time constants are increased. Typical power consumption is 1 mW per gate and switching time is 33 ns.

(iv) **74SXX (Schottky) series**   The speed of switching of heavily saturated bipolar transistors is limited due to the problem of excess stored charge carriers. If transistors are operated on the edge of saturation, however, the number of excess stored charge carriers is considerably reduced and faster switching times are possible. This mode of operation may be implemented with the aid of **Schottky barrier diodes (SBD).**

A Schottky diode consists of a semiconductor to metal interface rather than a p-n junction and therefore only one type of charge carrier is involved. This means that Schottky diodes do not suffer from charge carrier storage effects. In addition, Schottky diodes can be manufactured with a lower forward volt-drop (400 mV) than that encountered with p-n junction diodes (700 mV).

A typical switching circuit with the addition of a Schottky diode is shown in *Fig 19*. In this circuit, when TR1 is saturated, the volt-drop across the base-collector junction is limited to 400 mV by a forward biased Schottky diode (SBD). The Schottky diode has the effect of diverting the surplus base current, thus holding TR1 at the edge of saturation and

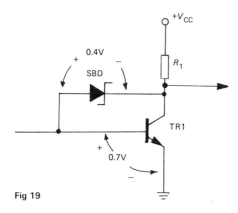

Fig 19

preventing the built up of excess stored charge carriers in the transistor. As a result of this, and due to the fact that a Schottky diode does not suffer from storage effects, the switching speed is greatly increased.

The circuit depicted in *Fig 19* may be implemented using Schottky transistors, and the simplified construction of such a transistor is shown in *Fig 20*. The Schottky diode is formed by extending the base contact over the collector region to form a semiconductor to metal interface. This type of transistor may be used to construct Schottky TTL circuits which have the advantage of higher switching speeds without the penalty of excessively increased power consumption. Typical power consumption of a Schottky TTL circuit is 20 mW per gate with a switching time of 3 ns.

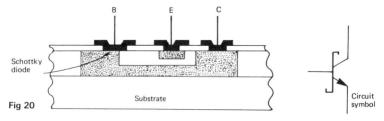

Fig 20

(v) **74LSXX series** This is a low power Schottky TTL family in which Schottky transistors are used to compensate for the reduced switching speeds that would otherwise occur when increasing resistor values throughout to obtain low power consumption. This logic family therefore has switching speeds similar to standard TTL, but with power consumption similar to that of the 74LXX series. Typical power consumption is 2 mW per gate with a switching time of 10 ns.

Problem 11 Draw the circuit diagram of a CMOS inverter and explain its operation.

A CMOS inverter consists of a *p*-channel MOSFET and an *n*-channel MOSFET connected in series across a supply, as shown in *Fig 21*. The *n*-channel MOSFET (TR1) acts as a switch with the *p*-channel MOSFET (TR2) as its active load.

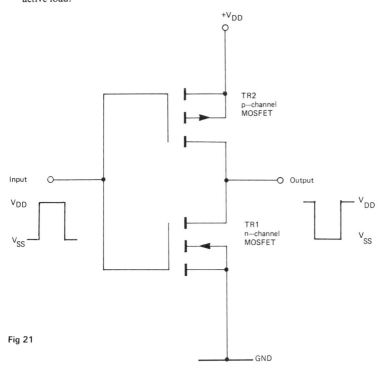

Fig 21

When the input to this circuit is held at logical 1, TR1 is biased into conduction and TR2 is biased to cut off, therefore the output is at logical 0 (0 V).

When the input is held at logical 0, TR1 is biased to cut off and TR2 is biased into conduction, therefore the output is at logical 1 ($+V_{DD}$).

Since FETs do not have base-emitter or saturation volt drops, the output voltage swing of an unloaded CMOS inverter is equal to the power supply voltage. This is illustrated by the CMOS inverter transfer characteristic shown in *Fig 22*.

It can be seen from this characteristic that changes in logic output level of a CMOS inverter take place at an input voltage of around 50% of the power supply potential.

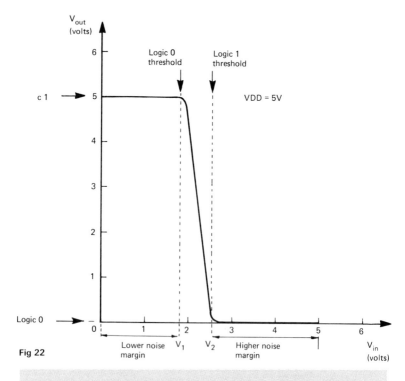

Fig 22

Problem 12 Draw the circuit diagram of a dual input CMOS NOR gate and explain its operation.

The circuit diagram of a CMOS NOR gate is illustrated in *Fig 23*. In this circuit, parallel connected transistors TR3 and TR4 act as the switching transistors with series connected TR1 and TR2 as their active load.

It can be seen from *Fig 23* that it is only possible to obtain an output of logical 1 if TR3 and TR4 are both cut off. An input of 0 V (logical 0) is required on both inputs A and B to achieve this condition, and this also causes TR1 and TR2 to conduct, thus pulling the output to $+V_{DD}$ (logical 1). All other input combinations cause TR3 or TR4 (or both) to conduct and TR1 or TR2 (or both) to cut off, thus giving an output of 0 V (logical 0).

Problem 13 Explain why care must be exercised in handling CMOS ICs, and list the main precautions to be observed.

The inputs of CMOS logic circuits are connected to the gates of MOSFETs and are insulated from the remainder of the circuit by a very thin layer of silicon

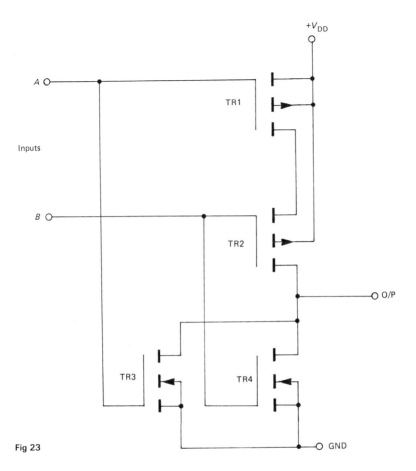

Fig 23

dioxide. Breakdown of this silicon dioxide layer and consequent destruction of the circuit occurs if a gate potential is allowed to rise above 50 V. Static charges of several thousand volts may build up on objects insulated from ground, and if this is allowed to happen with CMOS inputs, damage is inevitable.

CMOS inputs are usually protected against the build-up of static charges by the use of protection networks similar to that shown in *Fig 24*. Despite this, it is still advisable to observe the following precautions when handling CMOS ICs:

(i) always store CMOS ICs with their pins shorted together by embedding them in conductive foam or aluminium foil or use a special aluminium IC carrier,
(ii) do not remove ICs from their protective storage until required for insertion into a circuit,

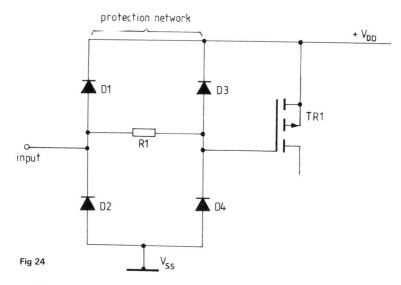

Fig 24

(iii) do not touch the pins of a CMOS IC,
(iv) do not install or remove a CMOS IC from circuit whilst it is powered,
(v) use a low leakage earthed soldering iron when installing CMOS ICs (better still — use IC sockets),
(vi) do not apply input signals to CMOS ICs when the power is disconnected,
(vii) do not leave CMOS IC inputs floating, and
(viii) avoid the use of materials which encourage the build-up of static electricity, e.g. nylon for clothing or working surfaces.

Problem 14 (i) Explain why CMOS ICs have low power consumption.
(ii) Show how power consumption in CMOS ICs varies with operating frequency.
(iii) Compare the power consumption of a standard TTL gate with that of a CMOS gate.

(i) The reason for CMOS circuits having low power consumption may be determined by considering a basic CMOS inverter circuit which forms the basis of all CMOS logic gates (see *Fig 25*). Under steady conditions, either TR1 or TR2 is non-conducting, depending upon the output logic level. Since MOSFETs have a very high resistance between source and drain when biased off, virtually no current flows in this circuit regardless of output logic level. The power consumption is therefore very low ($\approx 0.5\ \mu W$ per gate at 5 V, V_{DD}).

(ii) During an output transition from logical 0 to logical 1 (or vice versa), TR1 and TR2 are momentarily both conducting, and power consumption

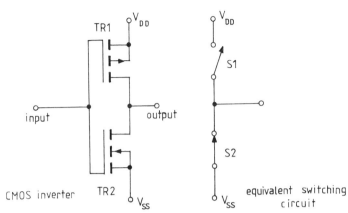

Fig 25

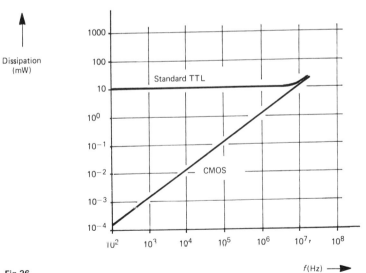

Fig 26

during this period is high. At low switching rates, the average power dissipated in a CMOS circuit is still very low, but as switching rates are increased power consumption rises, as shown in *Fig 26*.

(iii) In equivalent TTL circuits, at least one transistor is conducting at any instant in time, and therefore provides a current path across the supply at all times. For this reason, power consumption is relatively high under static conditions, and is largely independent of switching rate (see *Fig 26*), except when operating close to its maximum operating speed.

Problem 15 With the aid of a diagram, explain how:
(a) TTL outputs may be interfaced to CMOS inputs, and
(b) CMOS outputs may be interfaced to TTL inputs.

It is sometimes necessary to use a mixture of TTL and CMOS ICs for a given application. Interfacing TTL and CMOS circuits may be achieved by the following methods:

(a) *TTL output to CMOS input*
No problem exists in driving CMOS inputs directly from TTL outputs since they have greater output drive capabilities than CMOS outputs. The logical 1 output from a TTL circuit may not be high enough to drive a CMOS input, however, but this problem may be overcome by the use of a 2K2 'pull-up' resistor between the TTL output and $+V_{CC}$ (see *Fig 27*). This resistor ensures that the TTL logical 1 output rises to $+V_{CC}$ (5 V).

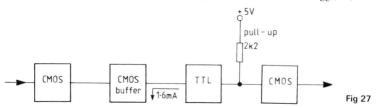

Fig 27

(b) *CMOS output to TTL input.*
The output circuit of a normal CMOS IC cannot sink a current of more than 0.5 mA. A standard TTL input requires that the circuit driving it is capable of sinking 1.6 mA. Therefore it is necessary to use a CMOS buffer with this drive capability between a standard CMOS output and a standard TTL input. An example of such a buffer is the type 4049 which is capable of driving two TTL loads.

Low power (74LXX) and low power Schottky (74LSXX) TTL circuits have much lower input current requirements (see problem 10) and these may be driven directly by normal CMOS outputs without further buffering.

Problem 16 Explain the difference between unbuffered (A series) and buffered (B series) CMOS circuits.

Table 2

INPUTS		STATE OF EACH TRANSISTOR				OUTPUT RESISTANCE
B	A	TR1	TR2	TR3	TR4	
0	0	ON	ON	OFF	OFF	TR1 & TR2 in series
0	1	OFF	ON	ON	OFF	TR3
1	0	ON	OFF	OFF	ON	TR4
1	1	OFF	OFF	ON	ON	TR3 & TR4 in parallel

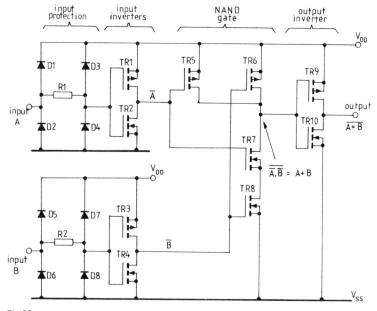

Fig 28

The circuit of an unbuffered CMOS NOR circuit is shown in *Fig 23*, and the state of each MOSFET in this circuit for all possible input conditions is shown in *Table 2*.

When conducting fully, MOSFETs do not behave as perfect switches, but have a resistance of several hundred ohms. Therefore, a CMOS gate has an output resistance of several hundred ohms, and as can be seen from *Table 2*, this varies in value according to its input conditions.

Each CMOS gate has an input capacitance of approximately 5pF which is formed by the capacitance between its gate electrode and the substrate. When two CMOS gates are interconnected, the output resistance of one gate and the input capacitance of the following gate behave as a low-pass filter which limits the maximum usable switching rate. Therefore, with unbuffered CMOS gates, the rise and fall times of the switching signals vary according to the particular input conditions present.

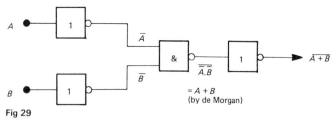

Fig 29

66

The circuit of a buffered CMOS NOR gate is shown in *Fig 28*. An inverter circuit, consisting of TR9 and TR10 is used to isolate or buffer the output terminal from the actual gate circuit output. This has the advantage of providing a constant output resistance, equivalent to the source to drain resistance of whichever MOSFET is conducting. Therefore the output resistance of a buffered CMOS gate does not vary according to its input conditions. Note that since the buffer causes inversion of the output logic level, the logic element used in *Fig 28* is a NAND gate with inverted inputs, i.e., a direct application of de Morgan's theorem is used. (See *Fig 29*).

Problem 17 Draw the circuit diagram of an emitter-coupled logic (ECL) OR/NOR gate.

The circuit diagram of an ECL OR/NOR gate is shown in *Fig 30*.

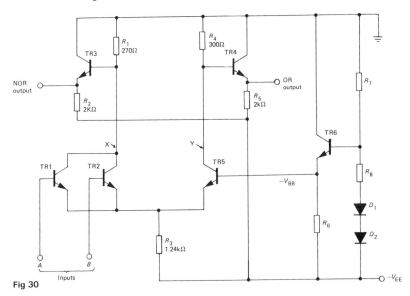

Fig 30

Problem 18 Describe the action of each transistor stage in *Fig 30*.

TR1, TR2 and TR3 form a basic ECL OR/NOR gate. When inputs A and B are both held at logical 0 ($-V_{EE}$), TR1 and TR2 are cut off and point X rises towards 0 V (logical 1). TR5 base-emitter junction is forward biased by $-V_{BB}$, therefore TR5 conducts and point Y falls towards $-V_{EE}$ (logical 0). A p.d. is developed across R_3 due to the current through TR5, and this is used to bias the emitters of TR1 and TR2.

If either TR1 or TR2 base (or both) is increased in potential towards 0V (logical 1), collector current flows and causes point X to fall towards $-V_{EE}$ (logical 0). The current through TR1 or TR2 (or both) causes extra current to flow through R_3 and the p.d. across this resistor increases. TR5 emitter potential rises towards $-V_{BB}$ and causes a reduction in its base-emitter potential. This causes TR5 to conduct less heavily and point Y rises towards 0V (logical 1). From this description it may be seen that point X behaves as a NOR output, and point Y behaves as an OR output.

TR3 and TR4 behave as output emitter followers. A problem arises if the ECL gate shown in *Fig 30* is used to drive the inputs of a similar ECL gate directly. The collectors of the driving transistors (points X and Y) are connected to the bases of similar circuits, which is clearly unacceptable. Emitter follower transistors TR3 and TR4 are used to shift the output voltage level to a value which is suitable for driving other ECL gates. The use of emitter followers also results in a low output impedance which improves the fan out capabilities of an ECL gate.

TR6 and its associated components form a bias compensating circuit. The noise margin of an ECL circuit may vary widely due to temperature variations, causing changes in circuit parameters. The effect can be minimised by using a temperature compensated supply for TR5 base $(-V_{BB})$.

An increase in temperature causes TR5 to conduct more heavily and changes the logic thresholds at inputs A and B. An increase in temperature also causes D1 and D2 to have a lower forward resistance, and this causes a decrease (more negative) in potential in TR6 base. This, in turn, causes a decrease in TR6 emitter potential $(-V_{BB})$, which offsets the change in conditions in the ECL circuit caused by the temperature increase. A temperature decrease has the opposite effect.

Problem 19 Explain the logic levels used in practical ECL circuits.

Transistors in ECL circuits do not saturate, but in order to obtain the maximum output voltage swing, it is desirable to operate between cut off and the edge of saturation (i.e. up to the point just before the collector-base junction becomes forward biased).

Typical voltages encountered in ECL circuits are:

$$V_{CC} = 0 \text{ V},$$
$$V_{EE} = -5.2 \text{ V}$$
$$V_{BB} = -1.15 \text{ V}$$

and $V_{BE_{SAT}} = 0.75 \text{ V}$.

The circuit diagram of part of an ECL gate circuit is shown in *Fig 31*. Using this circuit, various parameters may be calculated to determine the actual logic levels at its output terminal.

The logical 0 output condition, when TR5 is conducting heavily may first be considered:

(i) **p.d. across R_3,**

$$V_E = V_{EE} - (V_{BB} + V_{BE_{SAT}})$$
$$= 5.2 - (1.15 + 0.75) = \mathbf{3.3 \text{ V}}.$$

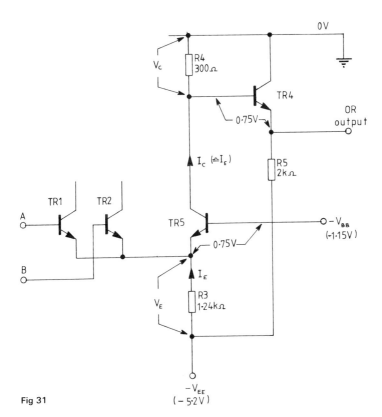

Fig 31

(ii) **Current through R_3,**

$$I_E = V_E/R_3$$

$$= \frac{3.3 \text{ V}}{1.24 \times 10^3} \text{ A} = \textbf{2.66 mA}.$$

If the gain of TR5 is high, such that $I_B \ll I_C$, it may be assumed that $I_C - I_E$, therefore,

(iii) **p.d. across R_4,**

$$V_C = I_E \times R_4$$
$$= 2.66 \times 10^{-3} \times 300 = \textbf{0.798 V}$$

(iv) **Output voltage,**

$$V_{OL} = 0 - V_C - V_{BE_{SAT}}$$
$$= 0 - 0.798 - 0.75 = \textbf{-1.55 V}$$

Therefore a logical 0 is represented at this gate output by a potential of approximately -1.55 V.

The logical 1 output condition, when TR5 is cut off may now be considered:
(i) I_E is diverted through one (or more) of the gate input transistors.
(ii) V_E rises towards $-V_{BB}$ and causes TR5 to cut off, causing I_C to become zero.
(iii) **p.d. across R_4**

$$V_C = I_B \times R_4.$$

but if the gain of TR6 is high, I_B is almost zero, therefore $V_C \approx 0$.

(iv) **Output voltage,**

$$V_{OL} = 0 - V_{BE_{SAT}} = \mathbf{-0.75\,V}$$

Therefore a logical 1 is represented at this gate output by a potential of approximately −0.75 V.

Using the values just calculated, it can be seen that an output voltage swing of 800 mV results when switching from logical 0 to logical 1 or vice versa.

Problem 20 Construct a table to compare TTL, CMOS and ECL gate circuits in terms of:
(a) logic swing (5V supply); (b) fan out; (c) power dissipation; and (d) propogation delay.

Table 3

	Standard TTL	Schottky TTL	LS TTL	ECL	CMOS
Logic swing	3.8 V	3.8 V	3.8 V	0.8 V	5 V
Fan out	10	10	10	25	50*
Power dissipation	10 mW	20 mW	2 mW	25 mW	10 nW
Propagation delay	10 nS	3 nS	10 nS	2 nS	50 nS

* lower for faster switching rates

C. FURTHER PROBLEMS ON LOGIC FAMILIES

(a) SHORT ANSWER PROBLEMS

1 The name given to a type of logic circuit which makes use of multiple-emitter transistors is . . . . . .

2 Logic circuits which make use of a mixture of *p*-channel and *n*-channel FETs are known as . . . . . . circuits.

3 A logic gate output stage which has its load resistor replaced by a transistor is said to have . . . . . .

4 A logic gate output stage which uses a transistor for its load is frequently known as a . . . . . . output stage.

5 Schottky transistors may be used in a TTL output stage to cause . . . . . .

6 For low power consumption, ... circuits are most likely to be used.

7 For very high speed switching, ... circuits are preferred.

8 If TTL gate outputs are connected in parallel, ... circuits must be used.

9 The current flowing in a TTL input when held at logical 0 is known as . . . . . ., and is equal to . . . . . . mA.

10 When driving a standard TTL input from a CMOS output, a . . . . . . circuit may be required.

11 When driving a CMOS input from a TTL output, a . . . . . . may be required.

12 Incorrect handling of CMOS circuits may cause them to be damaged by . . . . . .

13 TTL circuits must be operated with a supply of . . . . . .

14 CMOS circuits may be operated with a supply voltage between . . . . . . and . . . . . .

15 The power consumption of a CMOS logic circuit . . . . . . as the switching rate is increased.

16 The increase or decrease in potential at a gate input required to cause a change in logic output is known as the . . . . . . of the circuit.

17 The number of logic inputs that may be connected to a single output is known as the . . . . . . of a gate.

18 Unused TTL inputs should not be left floating, otherwise problems may arise due to . . . . . .

19 The main advantage of buffered, compared with unbuffered CMOS gates is that they have a constant . . . . . .

20 The power consumption of a standard TTL circuit is typically . . . . . . per gate.

21 The switching time for a standard TTL circuit is typically . . . . . .

22 The switching time for a low power Schottky (LS) circuit is typically . . . . . .

23 The switching time for a CMOS logic circuit is typically . . . . . .

24 The switching time for a Schottky TTL circuit is typically . . . . . .

25 The power consumption of an ECL gate circuit is typically . . . . . .

(b) CONVENTIONAL PROBLEMS

1 Explain two techniques used in TTL circuits to increase their operating speeds.

2 Explain why TTL circuits must operate with a 5 V supply, but CMOS circuits may be used with 3 V–15 V supplies.

3 Describe the factors which may limit the fan out of (a) TTL; (b) CMOS; and (c) ECL circuits.

4 Explain the term 'noise margin' when applied to logic circuits, and determine the noise margin of (a) TTL; (b) CMOS; and (c) ECL circuits when used with a 5 V supply.

5 State *two* applications where CMOS ICs may be used to advantage, and explain the particular advantages of CMOS over other forms of logic that makes it most appropriate for these applications.

6 Explain why input clamping diodes are used in (a) TTL and (b) CMOS circuits.

7 Draw the circuit diagram and explain the function of each component in a practical 'totem pole' output stage.

8 State *three* advantages of using ECL circuits and explain how each of these advantages is obtained.

9 Explain the problems associated with leaving unused inputs floating on (a) TTL and (b) CMOS circuits and show how these problems may be overcome.

10 Explain why, although the noise margin in ECL circuits is smaller than that for TTL circuits, ECL circuits are less likely to suffer from noise problems.

4 Bistables

A MAIN POINTS CONCERNED WITH BISTABLES

1 Logic circuits considered so far are of a type in which the output states are a function of the present inputs. The outputs of such circuits do not depend upon previous input or output conditions, i.e. they have no *'memory'* and they are known as *'combinational logic'* circuits. (See chapter 2.)

2 Logic circuits described in this chapter have memories, therefore their outputs are a function of previous inputs and outputs in addition to present inputs. These are known as *'sequential logic'* circuits, since they allow logical operations to be performed in sequence.

3 Sequential logic circuits may be *synchronous* or *asynchronous*. In synchronous sequential circuits, such output changes as are to take place all occur at the same instant in time under the control of a master pulse generator known as a *'system clock'*.
The outputs of asynchronous sequential circuits change state at random time intervals whenever their inputs are of such a value as to initiate changes.

4 The basic sequential logic circuit is called a *'bistable'* or *'flip-flop'* or *'latch'*, and it is a circuit whose output remains at a fixed logic level (0 or 1), until changed in response to an input signal. This circuit has two outputs called Q and $\bar{Q}$ (see *Fig 1*) and its condition is defined by the state of Q. Thus, if $Q = 0$, a bistable is defined as *'reset'*, and if $Q = 1$, a bistable is defined as *'set'*. $\bar{Q}$ represents the complementary state of a bistable.

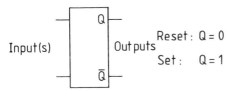

Fig 1

5 Many different forms of bistable are available, and the most commonly used types are
   (i) *R-S* bistable;   (iii) *D* bistable;
   (ii) clocked *R-S* bistable; (v) *J-K* bistable.

6 The *R-S bistable* is a basic, unclocked, bistable circuit which has two inputs, R (reset) and S (set). It derives its name from these two inputs and the state of its Q output is controlled directly by these two inputs (see *Fig 2*).

7 The *clocked R-S bistable* (see *Problems 1 to 3*) is a circuit that is more appropriate for use in synchronous circuits than the basic *R-S* bistable. Additional gate circuits are used at its inputs to prevent Q from responding to R and S until a clock pulse is applied. (See *Fig 3*.)

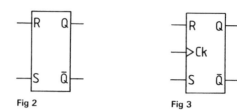

Fig 2   **Fig 3**

(See *Problems 5 and 6.*)

8 A *D-type bistable* is similar to a clocked *R-S* bistable in which the *R* and *S* inputs are combined to form a single *D* (data) input. This is achieved by connecting *R* to *S* through an inverter circuit, and using *S* as the *D* input (see *Fig 4*). This avoids the inconvenience of having to provide two data inputs as required by a clocked *R-S* bistable. When a *D*-type bistable is clocked, *Q* adopts the state of its *D* input.

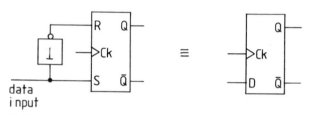

data input

Fig 4

(See *Problems 7 and 8.*)

9 A *T-type bistable* has a single *T* (toggle) input, and its *Q* output changes state in response to each input pulse at *T*. The *Q* output therefore changes at half the frequency of the input pulses, and the circuit behaves as a *binary divider* (see *Fig 5*).

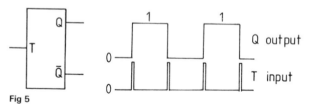

Fig 5

(see *Problem 9.*)

10 A *J-K bistable* is a universal or programmable bistable, similar in construction to a *T*-bistable, but with two additional inputs called *J* and *K* (to distinguish them from *R* and *S*). This type of bistable may function as a clocked *R-S* bistable or as a *T*-bistable, according to the inputs to *J* and *K*. This is illustrated in *Fig 6*.

(See *Problems 10 to 12.*)

11 A problem may arise when a bistable is used in the toggle mode (*T*-bistable)

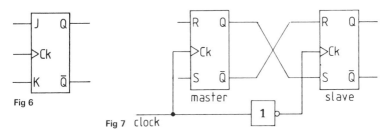

Fig 6

Fig 7 clock

due to its input clock pulse remaining active after the bistable changes state. This situation gives rise to unstable operation and causes oscillation to occur. This problem may be solved by always making sure that the clock pulse duration is equal to or shorter than a bistable switching time. This is not always convenient, however, and in these cases it may be preferable to use a *'master-slave'* circuit in which the clock pulse duration can be made independent of the bistable switching time. (See *Fig 7*.)

This circuit consists of two bistables, arranged such that the first (*the master*) drives the second (*the slave*). The clock inputs to the two bistables are arranged such that they cannot both be simultaneously enabled. Information may be clocked into the master (but not the slave) when a clock pulse is present, and transferred to the slave when the clock pulse is terminated. (See *Problem 16*).

B. WORKED PROBLEMS ON BISTABLES

Problem 1 Draw the logic block diagram of an *R-S* bistable using NOR gates and explain its operation.

An *R-S* bistable may be constructed from two cross-coupled NOR gates as shown in *Fig 8*. The action of this circuit may be described by considering the initial conditions to be:

$S = 0, R = 0, Q = 0, \overline{Q} = 1$

G_1 has its inputs at logical 0 and logical 1 respectively, and this maintains Q at logical 0. G_2 has a logical 0 on both its inputs and this maintains $\overline{Q}$ at logical 1. These conditions are stable and the bistable is in its *'reset'* condition.

If S is changed to logical 1, G_2 inputs are now logical 0 and logical 1 respectively, which causes $\overline{Q}$ to change to logical 0. Since $\overline{Q}$ is connected to one input of G_1, this gate now has logical 0 on both its inputs. Therefore Q changes to logical 1, which in turn is connected to one input of G_2 to hold $\overline{Q}$ at logical 0. This condition is steady and is maintained even if S returns to logical 0, and the bistable is in its *'set'* condition. If R is changed to logical 1, G_1 inputs are now logical 0 and logical 1, respectively, which causes Q to change to logical 0 and reverse the above process. The bistable is returned to its stable 'reset' condition. Note, the condition $S = R = 1$ is not permitted since this would force

75

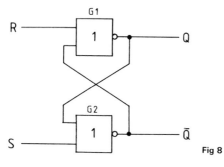

Fig 8

both Q and $\bar{Q}$ to logical 0 and the state of the bistable after S and R return to logical 0 is indeterminate.

Problem 2 Construct a truth table for the *R-S* bistable described in the answer to *Problem 1*.

Table 1

R	S	Q	Q^+	
0	0	0	0	
0	1	0→1		
1	0	0	0	
1	1	0	X	}indeterminate
0	0	1	1	
0	1	1	1	
1	0	1→0		
1	1	1	X	}indeterminate

Sequential circuit elements, such as bistables, have feedback, i.e. their outputs are connected back to their input circuits. For this reason, determining the state of a present output must take into account previous outputs as well as present inputs. To differentiate between present and previous outputs, Q indicates the previous state of an output, and Q^+ indicates the state of an output after it responds to the input conditions specified.

Using this notation, the truth table for an *R-S* bistable is shown in *Table 1*.

Problem 3 With the aid of a Karnaugh map, determine the logic equations for the *R-S* bistable described in *Problem 1*.

The logical equation for an *R-S* bistable may be derived from its truth table (*Table 1*). Since the condition $S = R = 1$ is not allowed, this may be treated as a '*don't care*' condition for the purpose of deriving the logical equations (i.e. this condition may be considered as either a logical 0 or logical 1 and this is indicated by an 'X').

The equations are:

(i) $Q^+ = (\overline{R}.\overline{S}.Q + \overline{R}.S.Q + \overline{R}.S.\overline{Q})_1 + (R.S.Q + R.S.\overline{Q})_x$
    '1' terms   'don't care' terms

(ii) $Q^+ = (\overline{R}.\overline{S}.\overline{Q} + R.\overline{S}.\overline{Q} + R.\overline{S}.Q)_0 + (R.S.Q + R.S.\overline{Q})_x$
    '1' terms   'don't care' terms

Karnaugh maps for these equations are shown in *Figs 9(a) and (b)*.

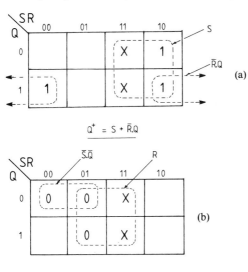

Fig 9

Simplifying equations (i) and (ii) using these Karnaugh maps gives the following expressions for Q^+ and $\overline{Q}^+$:

$$Q^+ = S + \overline{R}.Q,$$
and $$\overline{Q}^+ = R + \overline{S}.\overline{Q}.$$

Problem 4 Draw the logic block diagram of a $\overline{R}$-$\overline{S}$ bistable using NAND gates and describe its operations.

A $\overline{R}$-$\overline{S}$ bistable may be constructed from two cross-coupled NAND gates as shown in *Fig 10*. The action of this circuit may be described by considering the initial conditions to be:

$\overline{S} = 1, \overline{R} = 1, Q = 0, \overline{Q} = 1$

G_1 has a logical 1 on both of its inputs and this maintains Q at a logical 0.
G_2 has its inputs at logical 0 and logical 1 respectively, and this maintains $\overline{Q}$ at
logical 1. These conditions are stable, and the bistable is in its *'reset'* condition.

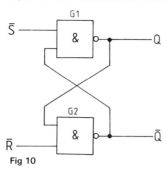

Fig 10

If $\overline{S}$ is changed to logical 0, G_1 inputs are now logical 1 and logical 0 respectively, which causes Q to change to a logical 1. Since Q is connected to one input of G_2, this gate now has a logical 1 on both its inputs. Therefore, $\overline{Q}$ changes to logical 0, which, in turn is connected to one input of G_1 to hold Q at logical 1. This condition is stable, and is maintained even if $\overline{S}$ returns to logical 1, and the bistable is in its *'set'* condition.

Q may be changed back to a logical 0 by applying a logical 0 to $\overline{R}$ which reverses the above process.

Note, the condition $\overline{R} = \overline{S} = 0$ is not permitted since this would force both Q and $\overline{Q}$ to logical 0 and the state of the bistable after $\overline{S}$ and $\overline{R}$ return to logical 1 is indeterminate.

Problem 5 Draw the logic block diagram of a clocked *R-S* bistable using NAND gates and describe its operation.

The circuit of a clocked *R-S* bistable constructed from NAND gates is shown in *Fig 11*.

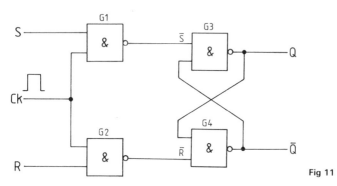

Fig 11

G_3 and G_4 act as a $\overline{R}$-$\overline{S}$ bistable of the type described in *Problem 4*.
G_1 and G_2 act as input gates to inhibit the R and S inputs until the Ck input becomes active (logic 1) and to ensure that all changes take place in synchronism with a system clock.

Therefore, if $S = 1$ and $Ck = 1$, a logical 0 is applied to $\overline{S}$ and this causes Q to become logical 1 (bistable set). If $R = 1$ and $Ck = 1$, a logical 0 is applied to $\overline{R}$ and this causes Q to become logical 0 (bistable reset). The condition $S = 1$, $R = 1$ and $Ck = 1$ is not permitted.

Problem 6 Construct a truth table for the clocked *R-S* bistable described in *Problem 5*, and use this truth table to derive its logic equations.

The truth table for a clocked *R-S* is shown in *Table 2*. Observation of this table shows that when Ck input is active (logical 1), the circuit behaves as an ordinary *R-S* bistable, but when the clock is inactive (logical 0), Q remains unchanged for all input combinations of R and S. From *Table 2*, the equation

Table 2

S	R	Ck	Q	Q⁺	
0	0	0	0	0	clock inactive
0	1	0	0	0	
1	0	0	0	0	
1	1	0	0	0	
0	0	0	1	1	
0	1	0	1	1	
1	0	0	1	1	
1	1	0	1	1	
0	0	1	0	0	clock active
0	1	1	0	0	
1	0	1	0→1		
1	1	1	0	X	indeterminate
0	0	1	1	1	
0	1	1	1→0		
1	0	1	1	1	
1	1	1	1	X	indeterminate

79

for Q^+ may be obtained, and this is:

$$Q^+ = (\bar{S}.\bar{R}.\overline{Ck}.Q + \bar{S}.R.\overline{Ck}.Q + S.\bar{R}.\overline{Ck}.Q + S.R.\overline{Ck}.Q + S.\bar{R}.Ck.Q + \bar{S}.\bar{R}.Ck.Q$$
$$+ S.\bar{R}.Ck + Q)_1 + (S.R.Ck.\bar{Q} + S.R.Ck.Q)_x$$

'1' terms   'don't care' terms

Similarly, an expression for $\bar{Q}^+$ may be obtained, and this is:

$$\bar{Q}^+ = (\bar{S}.\bar{R}.\overline{Ck}.\bar{Q} + \bar{S}.R.\overline{Ck}.\bar{Q} + S.\bar{R}.\overline{Ck}.\bar{Q} + S.R.\overline{Ck}.\bar{Q} + \bar{S}.R.Ck.\bar{Q} + \bar{S}.R.Ck.\bar{Q} + \bar{S}.R.Ck.Q)_0 + (S.R.Ck.\bar{Q} + S.R.Ck.Q)_x$$

'0' terms   'don't care' terms

The expression for Q^+ is entered on the Karnaugh map shown in *Fig 12(a)* and the expression for $\bar{Q}^+$ is entered on the Karnaugh map shown in *Fig 12(b)*.

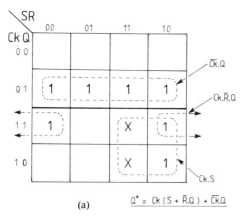

(a) $Q^+ = Ck(S + \bar{R}.Q) + \overline{Ck}.Q$

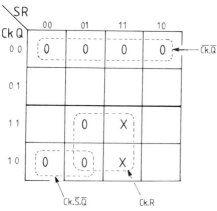

Fig 12   (b) $\bar{Q}^+ = Ck(R + \bar{S}.\bar{Q}) + \overline{Ck}.\bar{Q}$

By means of the normal map simplification methods, the following equations are obtained:

(i) $Q^+ = Ck.S + Ck.\overline{R}.Q + \overline{Ck}.Q$
    $= Ck(S + \overline{R}.Q) + \overline{Ck}.Q$

(ii) $\overline{Q}^+ = Ck.R + Ck.\overline{S}.\overline{Q} + \overline{Ck}.\overline{Q}$
    $= Ck(R + \overline{S}.\overline{Q}.) + \overline{Ck}.\overline{Q}$

It can be seen from these equations that if Ck is active (logical 1), the expressions for Q^+ and $\overline{Q}^+$ are identical to those derived in *Problem 3* for the ordinary R-S bistable. If Ck is inactive (logical 0), the expressions for Q^+ and $\overline{Q}^+$ indicate that Q remains unchanged.

Problem 7 Draw the logic block diagram of a *D*-type bistable, using NAND gates, and explain its operation.

The circuit of a *D*-type bistable, constructed from NAND gates, is shown in *Fig 13(a)*.

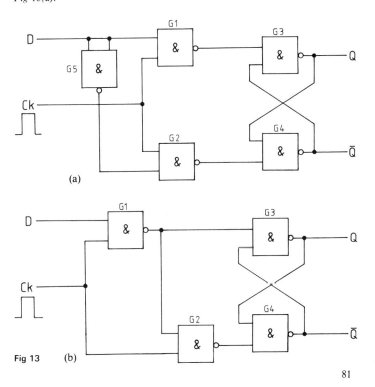

Fig 13

Gates G_1 to G_4 behave as a clocked *R-S* bistable of the type described in *Problem 5*, except that its *R* and *S* inputs are combined into a single *D* input by means of G_5 which acts as an inverter stage. The inverter stage ensures that *R* and *S* are always at opposite logic levels (i.e. the forbidden input condition $R = S = 1$ cannot occur), and also avoids the inconvenience of having to provide two separate input signals.

This circuit may be simplified so that only four gates are necessary. The output from G_1 is logical 1 when the *D* input is logical 0 and logical 0 when the *D* input is logical 1 during the active clock period ($Ck = 1$). Therefore since the output of G_1 is always the complement of *D* (i.e. $\overline{D}$), this may be used as an input for G_2. This circuit arrangement is illustrated in *Fig 13(b)*.

Note, with this type of circuit, *Q* follows *D* when the clock is active (logical 1), and latching takes place on the trailing edge of each clock pulse (see *Fig 14*).

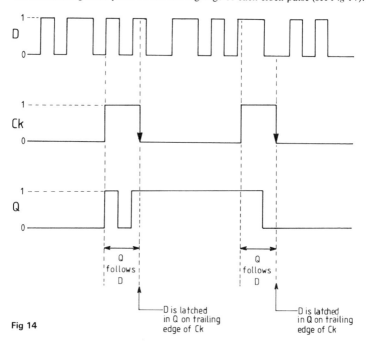

Fig 14

Problem 8 Construct the truth table for a *D*-type bistable, and, with the aid of Karnaugh maps, derive its logic equations.

The truth table for a *D*-type bistable is shown in *Table 3*. From this truth table the equations for Q^+ and $\overline{Q}^+$ may be derived, and these are:

(i) $Q^+ = \overline{D}.\overline{Ck}.Q + D.\overline{Ck}.Q + D.Ck.\overline{Q} + D.Ck.Q$, and
(ii) $\overline{Q}^+ = \overline{D}.\overline{Ck}.\overline{Q} + D.\overline{Ck}.\overline{Q} + \overline{D}.Ck.\overline{Q} + \overline{D}.Ck.Q$

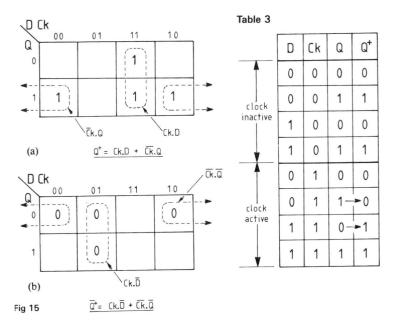

Fig 15

Karnaugh maps for these equations are shown in *Figs 15(a) and (b)*.

Simplifying equations (i) and (ii) using these Karnaugh maps gives the following expressions for Q^+ and $\overline{Q}^+$:

$$Q^+ = Ck.D + \overline{Ck}.Q,$$
and $$\overline{Q}^+ = Ck.\overline{D} + \overline{Ck}.\overline{Q}.$$

It can be seen from these equations, that when the clock is active (logical 1), $Q^+ = D$ and $\overline{Q}^+ = \overline{D}$. When the clock is inactive (logical 0) no changes take place.

Problem 9 Draw the logic block diagram of a *T*-type bistable using NAND gates and describe its operation.

A *T*-type bistable may be constructed from a clocked *R-S* bistable by applying feedback from Q to R and from $\overline{Q}$ to S, (see *Fig 16*). The clock input acts as a *T* (toggle) input, with Q and $\overline{Q}$ priming R and S so that the bistable alternates between its 'set' and 'reset' conditions in response to each input pulse at *T*. For example, suppose the bistable shown in *Fig 16* is initially in its reset condition, i.e. $Q = 0$, $\overline{Q} = 1$. Because of the feedback from Q and $\overline{Q}$, it follows that $R = 0$ and $S = 1$, and these input conditions are such as to cause the bistable to be set upon arrival of the next input pulse at *T*. Therefore, Q and $\overline{Q}$ change state to become logical 1 and logical 0 respectively, and this change is

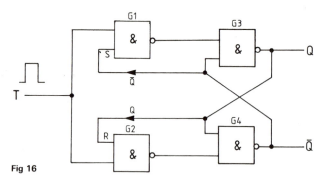

Fig 16

fed back to R and S, such that $R = 1$ and $S = 0$. These input conditions cause the bistable to reset upon arrival of the next input pulse at T.

This process is repeated with the effect that Q alternates (toggles) between logical 0 and logical 1 in response to each input pulse at T.

Problem 10 Draw the logical block diagram of a *J-K* bistable using NAND gates and describe its operation.

The block diagram of a *J-K* bistable constructed from NAND gates is shown in *Fig 17*. This circuit is basically the same as the *T*-type bistable shown in *Fig 16*, except for the provision of an additional input to each of the clock gating circuits G_1 and G_2. These additional inputs are called J and K (to distinguish them from S and $\bar{R}$), and they enable a more versatile bistable circuit to be constructed.

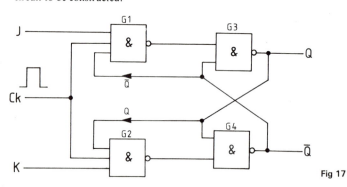

Fig 17

The operation of a *J-K* bistable may be studied by considering the following input conditions on J and K:

(i) $J = K = 0$.

Since G_1 and G_2 each have at least one input at logical 0 under these

84

conditions, their outputs are both held at logical 1 regardless of the state of the clock input or the Q and $\overline{Q}$ feedback signals. Since G_3 and G_4 form a $\overline{R}$-$\overline{S}$ bistable, a change from logical 1 to logical 0 is required at $\overline{R}$ or $\overline{S}$ to cause any change in Q and $\overline{Q}$. Therefore, under these conditions, no change in output can take place.

(ii) $J \neq K$ (i.e. $J = 0$, $K = 1$ or $J = 1$, $K = 0$).

If the input conditions are such that $J = 1$ and $K = 0$ and the bistable is in the reset condition ($Q = 0$, $\overline{Q} = 1$), the arrival of a clock pulse causes all three inputs to G_1 to be at logical 1. This causes G_1 output to change to logical 0 and set the bistable. Once in the set condition, the output of G_1 remains at logical 1 due to the feedback from $\overline{Q}$. If the input conditions are such that $J = 0$ and $K = 1$ and the bistable is in the set condition ($Q = 1$, $\overline{Q} = 0$), the arrival of a clock pulse causes all three inputs to G_2 to be at logical 1. This causes G_2 to be at logical 1. This causes G_2 output to change to logical 0 and reset the bistable. Once in the reset condition, the output of G_2 remains at logical 1 due to feedback from Q.

(iii) $J = K = 1$.

This condition, which is forbidden in a clocked R-S bistable, is permitted with a J-K bistable. Its effect is to make the outputs of G_1 and G_2, when clocked, dependent solely upon the logic levels fed back from Q and $\overline{Q}$, i.e. the circuit effectively becomes the same as the T-type bistable shown in *Fig 16*. Therefore the condition $J = K = 1$ causes a J-K bistable to behave as a T-type bistable, and Q alternates between logical 0 and logical 1 in response to each clock pulse.

Therefore a J-K bistable may be considered to behave as a clocked R-S bistable unless $J = K = 1$ when it behaves as a T-type bistable.

Problem 11 Construct the truth table for a J-K bistable, and, with the aid of Karnaugh maps, derive its logic equations.

The truth table for a J-K bistable is shown in *Table 4*. From this truth table, the equations for Q^+ and $\overline{Q}^+$ may be derived, and these are:

(i) $Q^+ = \bar{J}.\bar{K}.\overline{Ck}.Q + \bar{J}.K.\overline{Ck}.Q + J.\bar{K}.\overline{Ck}.Q + J.K.\overline{Ck}.Q +$
$\quad J.\bar{K}.Ck.\overline{Q} + J.K.Ck.\overline{Q} + \bar{J}.\bar{K}.Ck.Q + J.\bar{K}.Ck.Q.$

(ii) $\overline{Q}^+ = \bar{J}.\bar{K}.\overline{Ck}.\overline{Q} + \bar{J}.K.\overline{Ck}.\overline{Q} + J.\bar{K}.\overline{Ck}.\overline{Q} + J.K.\overline{Ck}.\overline{Q} +$
$\quad \bar{J}.\bar{K}.Ck.\overline{Q} + \bar{J}.K.Ck.\overline{Q} + \bar{J}.K.Ck.Q + J.K.Ck.Q.$

Karnaugh maps for these equations are shown in *Figs 18(a) and (b)*.

Simplifying equations (i) and (ii) using these Karnaugh maps gives the following expressions for Q^+ and $\overline{Q}^+$:

$Q^+ = Ck(J.\overline{Q} + \overline{K}.Q) + \overline{Ck}.Q,$
$\overline{Q}^+ = Ck(\bar{J}.\overline{Q} + K.\overline{Q}) + Ck.Q.$

Table 4

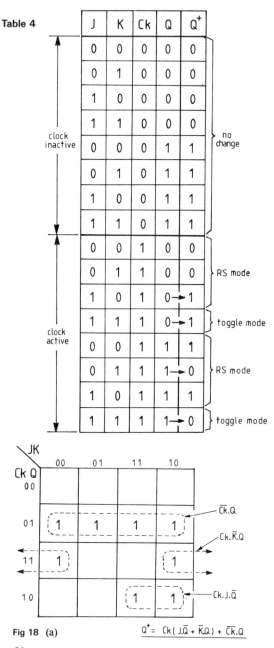

Fig 18 (a)

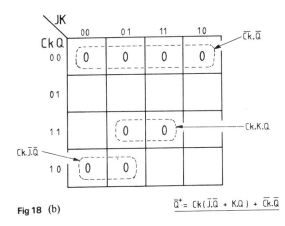

Fig 18 (b)

$$\overline{Q}^+ = Ck(\overline{J}.\overline{Q} + K.Q) + \overline{Ck}.\overline{Q}$$

Problem 12 Explain why a *T*-type bistable (or a *J-K* bistable operated as a *T*-type bistable) may operate in an unstable manner and state how this problem may be overcome.

A *T*-type bistable (or a *J-K* bistable operated in the toggle mode, i.e. $J = K = 1$) normally operates such that a single change in state of its Q output occurs for each input clock pulse, as shown in *Fig 19(a)*.

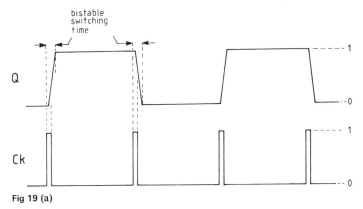

Fig 19 (a)

A different situation arises if the duration of each clock pulse is made much longer than the time taken for the bistable to change state. In this case, the bistable changes state continuously for the duration of the clock pulse. This is an unstable form of operation, called *'oscillation'* and is shown in *Fig 19(b)*. The final state of Q is unpredictable, and depends upon the duration of the clock pulse and the frequency of oscillation.

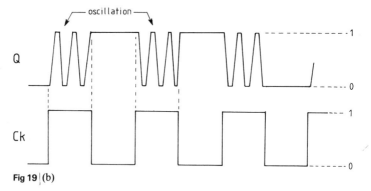

Fig 19 (b)

The problem of unstable operation in *T*-type bistables may be overcome by one of the following methods:

(i) use clock pulses which are of shorter duration than the bistable switching time,
(ii) use of a bistable with *'edge triggering'* (see *Problems 13 and 14*), or
(iii) use of a *'master-slave'* bistable (see *Problem 16*).

Problem 13 Explain the difference between an edge triggered bistable and a level triggered bistable.

Most bistables are clocked circuits which do not respond immediately to changes in input conditions, but which change state only after the application of a clocking pulse.

The term 'triggering' has the same meaning as 'clocking' and refers to the effect of applying a single clock pulse at the *Ck* input.

Bistables may be triggered by either positive or negative clock pulses (see

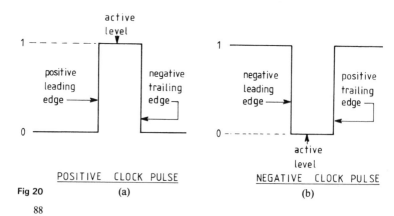

Fig 20   (a)   (b)

Figs 20(a) and (b)). A bistable may respond to a clock pulse in one of three different ways:

(i) *positive edge triggering* A bistable with this type of triggering changes state in response to its inputs when a logical 0 to logical 1 transition occurs on its *Ck* input.
(ii) *negative edge triggering* A bistable with this type of triggering changes state in response to its inputs when a logical 1 to logical 0 transition occurs on its *Ck* input.
(iii) *level triggering* A bistable with this type of triggering changes state in response to its inputs all the time that the clock input is held at an active level, i.e. logical 0 or logical 1 depending upon the type of bistable.

Problem 14 Explain how a bistable may be constructed so that it responds to edge triggering.

A bistable clock input may be made edge sensitive by including a *CR* network (differentiator) in series with the clock signal path, as shown in *Fig 21(a)*. A differentiator circuit generates an output only when its input voltage is changing, as shown in *Fig 21(b)* (the negative part of its output may be removed by an appropriate diode clipping circuit). If the *CR* time constant is made very short, the bistable then appears to respond to the leading edge only of the applied clock pulse.

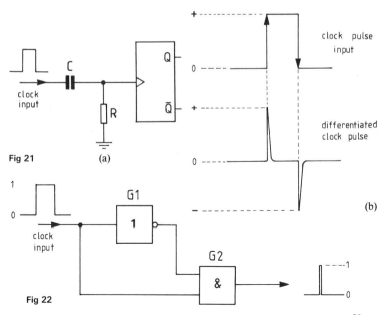

Fig 21

Fig 22

89

A *CR* network is not always the most convenient circuit for use in integrated circuits, and a propagation delay circuit of the type shown in *Fig 22* may be used instead.

Theoretically, the output from G_2 should remain at logical 0 in this circuit, due to the action of G_1 keeping both inputs to G_2 at different logic levels. In practice, due to the propagation delay in G_1, when the clock input changes from logical 0 to logical 1, both inputs to G_2 are momentarily held at logical 1. This causes G_2 to produce a very short duration output pulse to cause triggering of the bistable. This pulse is only generated on the leading edge of the clock input, as shown in *Fig 23,* therefore the bistable only responds to the positive edge of the clock pulse.

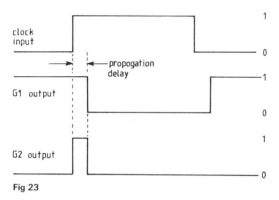

Fig 23

Problem 15 (i) Explain the function of PRESET and CLEAR inputs on a bistable. (ii) Explain the difference between synchronous and asynchronous CLEAR inputs.

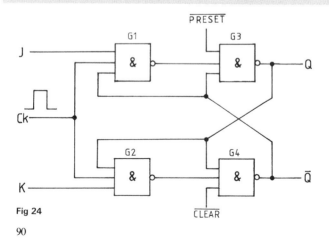

Fig 24

90

(i) PRESET and CLEAR inputs may be either active high or active low, and they behave in a similar manner to SET and RESET on an *R-S* bistable. When an active level is applied to the PRESET input of a bistable, its Q output takes up a logical 1 state, and when an active level is applied to the CLEAR input of a bistable, its Q output takes up a logical 0 state. These inputs override all other inputs and cause instantaneous changes in Q output.

The PRESET and CLEAR inputs to a typical *J-K* bistable are arranged as shown in *Fig 24*. These are both 'active low' inputs, i.e. a logical 0 is required to cause the preset or clear action.

(ii) In most bistable circuits, the CLEAR input overrides all other inputs, i.e. it is an *'asynchronous clear'*. Some bistable circuits do not respond to an active level on the CLEAR input until the arrival of the next clock pulse. These bistables have *'synchronous clear'* inputs.

Problem 16 Draw the logic circuit of a 'master-slave' *J-K* bistable, and briefly explain its operation.

The logic circuit of a master slave *J-K* bistable is shown in *Fig 25*. NAND gates G_1 to G_4 form a master *J-K* bistable circuit, and G_5 to G_8 form a closed *R-S* slave bistable.

When *Ck* is at logical 1, data may be clocked into the master bistable, but not into the slave bistable, since G_9 holds the slave clocking signal ($\overline{Ck}$) at logical 0. At the end of the clock pulse period, *Ck* returns to logical 0, and $\overline{Ck}$ becomes logical 1 which allows data to be clocked into the slave from the master outputs Q' and $\overline{Q}'$.

Feedback takes place from the slave outputs Q and $\overline{Q}$ to the master input gates, but a complete feedback path is not maintained, since only the master or the slave (not both) is clocked at any instant. Therefore, when this type of bistable is used in the toggle mode ($J = K = 1$), instability cannot occur and the duration of the clock pulse is therefore relatively unimportant.

Problem 17 Describe a simple application for the $\overline{R}\text{-}\overline{S}$ bistable.

A $\overline{R}\text{-}\overline{S}$ bistable may be used to overcome the problem of contact bounce associated with mechanical switches. When a mechanical switch is operated, its contacts do not make cleanly, but bounce for a period of 10-20 ms before finally coming to rest. This action is illustrated in *Fig 26*.

Logic circuits operate at very high speeds, and when a mechanical switch is connected to such circuits, switch bounce is interpreted as several individual switch closures. A system for preventing a logic circuit from responding to switch bounce is therefore necessary, and this is known as **'switch debouncing'**. A $\overline{R}\text{-}\overline{S}$ bistable of the type described in *Problem 4* may be used to debounce a mechanical switch, as shown in *Fig 27*.

When S1 is operated so that it moves to position 'A', the Q output rises to logical 1, but cannot return to logical 0 until S1 contacts position 'B'. When S1

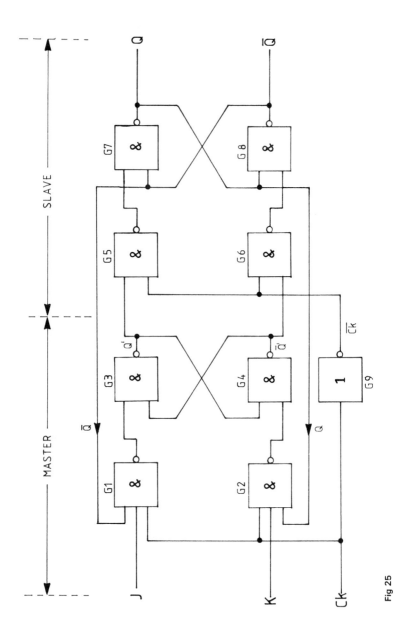

Fig 25

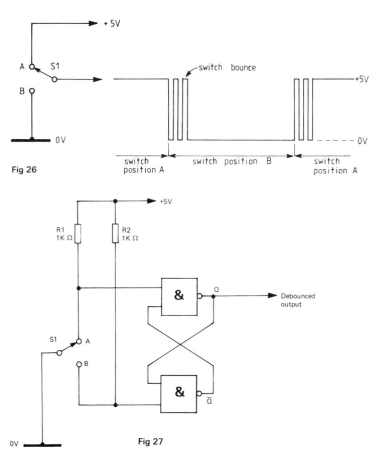

Fig 26

Fig 27

bounces, it does so against the contact at 'A', but with insufficient movement to contact 'B' again. The reverse is also true when S1 is moved from 'A' back to 'B' and Q changes from logical 1 back to logical 0. Therefore Q changes cleanly from one logic level to another without the effects of switch bounce.

C FURTHER PROBLEMS ON BISTABLES

(a) SHORT ANSWER PROBLEMS

1 Logic circuits whose outputs are a function of their present inputs are known as ..... circuits.

2 Logic circuits whose outputs are a function of previous outputs in addition to present inputs are known as . . . . . . circuits.

3 Logic circuits whose output changes occur in step with a system master clock are known as . . . . . . circuits.

4 In an R-S bistable circuit, the input condition $R = \ldots \ldots, S = \ldots \ldots$ should *not* be used.

5 The two output terminals of a bistable circuit are usually called . . . . . . and . . . . . .

6 The output of a T-type bistable changes at . . . . . . of its input clock frequency.

7 A J-K bistable may operate in the toggle mode if the input conditions are $J = \ldots \ldots$ and $K = \ldots \ldots$

8 A clocked R-S bistable which has its R and S inputs combined into a single input is known as a . . . . . . bistable.

9 A circuit which consists of two bistables connected in series with alternate clocking of each bistable is known as a . . . . . . bistable.

10 Three types of triggering used for bistable circuits are known as . . . . and . . . . . . triggering.

11 In order to avoid problems with instability, a T-type bistable may use . . . . . . triggering.

12 Two inputs to a bistable which may be used to set or reset it and which override all other inputs are called . . . . . . and . . . . . .

(b) CONVENTIONAL PROBLEMS

1 Draw the logic block diagram of a clocked R-S bistable constructed from NOR gates only.

2 Construct a truth table for a $\overline{R}$-$\overline{S}$ bistable, and, using mapping methods derive its logic equations.

3 With the aid of diagrams, show how a J-K bistable may be connected so that it operates as:
(a) a clocked R-S bistable; (b) a D-type bistable; (c) a T-type bistable.
Briefly explain how each circuit provides the required function.

4 With the aid of a diagram, explain how a D-type bistable can be made to function as a binary divider.

5 A motor control circuit is operated by means of three momentary action push-button switches, one each for 'forwards', 'reverse' and 'stop'. Draw a logic block diagram to show how bistable circuits may be used to construct a suitable controller.

6 An electronic system is required for a workshop to control four machines. Each machine is fitted with separate 'on' and 'off' buttons, and a wall-mounted master switch is provided to turn off all machines in the case of an emergency (all switches are of the momentary action 'push-to-make' type).
Draw a logic block diagram, using J-K bistables, of a suitable control system.

5 Counters

A MAIN POINTS CONCERNED WITH COUNTERS

1 A binary counter may be defined as a group of interconnected bistables, having a single input, and arranged such that they indicate (in binary) the total number of pulses applied to the input (see *Fig 1*). In order to perform a counting function, the bistables in *Fig 1* must be operated as binary dividers. When operated in this mode, a bistable requires two input pulses to generate a single pulse at its Q output. A *J-K* bistable may be used as a binary divider if both its J and K inputs are connected to a logical 1 level (see *Fig 2*).

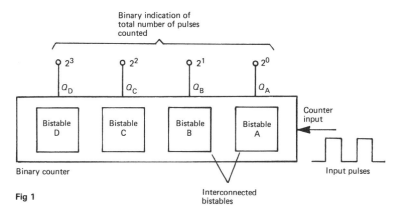

Fig 1

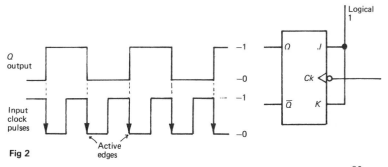

Fig 2

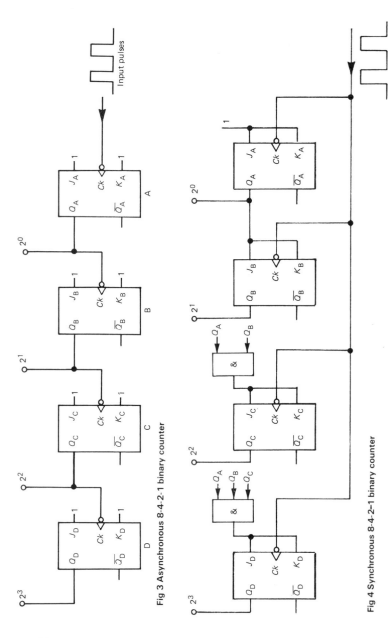

Fig 3 Asynchronous 8-4-2-1 binary counter

Fig 4 Synchronous 8-4-2-1 binary counter

It was shown in chapter 4, *Problem 10,* that when a *J-K* bistable is operated as in *Fig 2,* its Q output changes state on every active edge of its clock input. Since each clock pulse has only one active edge, two input pulses are necessary to cause Q to change state from a logical 0 to a logical 1 and back again.

2 Binary counters may be classified as: (a) **asynchronous** (or serial); or (b) **synchronous** (or parallel).

An asynchronous counter is arranged such that each stage in the counter, except the first, is clocked by the output from the preceding stage. The first stage is clocked by the input pulses being counted. A counter of this type is illustrated in *Fig 3*. Each input pulse causes Q_A to change state, and if this change represents an active edge, stage B is clocked as a consequence, and Q_B changes state. This action is repeated between the remaining stages of the counter, and hence changes ripple through the counter from stage A to stage D. Due to propogation delays, the Q output of each stage changes state a short time after the arrival of an active clock edge. Thus the bistables in this type of counter do not change state in synchronism, but one after another, i.e. asynchronously. An asynchronous counter is also known as a **'ripple-through'** counter.

Although asynchronous counters are simple in construction, they have the following disadvantages:

(i) a relatively long time is required to set up each new count due to the ripple-through effect caused by the accumulative effect of the individual propogation delays;

(ii) the maximum counting rate is limited because of the effects in (i); and

(iii) transitional counts (dynamic hazards) are generated. (See *Problem 2.*)

3 A synchronous counter is arranged such that all bistables in the counter are clocked in synchronism by a common clock signal. Hence, all bistables in a synchronous counter which must change state to progress from one stage in a count to the next, do so simultaneously. The J and K inputs of all stages in a synchronous counter are pre-conditioned prior to clocking so that their Q outputs progress to the next sequence of the count after clocking. A typical synchronous counter using *J-K* bistables is shown in *Fig 4*.

A synchronous counter is more complex than an asynchronous counter, but has the following advantages:

(i) the time required to set up each new count is reduced to the propogation time for a single bistable,

(ii) the maximum counting rate is increased because of (i), and (iii) there are no transitional counts.

4 In a 4-bit pure binary counter, the number of input pulses required to change the state of Q_D, Q_C, Q_B and Q_A are 8, 4, 2 and 1 respectively. Thus a logical 1 on Q_D has a different value or weight to a logical 1 on, say, Q_A. These are called **'weighted'** counters, and are frequently known as 8-4-2-1 pure binary counters.

5 A truth table, which shows the states of the Q and $\overline{Q}$ outputs of an 8-4-2-1 pure binary asynchronous counter as the counting sequence proceeds, is presented in *Table 1*. By observation of columns 1 to 4 (the Q outputs) it can be seen that the arrival of each input pulse causes the count to be increased by 1. This type of count is known as an **'up count'**. Observation of columns 5 to 8 (the $\overline{Q}$ outputs) shows that the arrival of each input pulse causes the count to be decreased by 1, i.e. a **'down count'** is obtained. Therefore, by selecting the Q outputs of this counter, an up count from 0 to 15 may be obtained and by selecting the $\overline{Q}$ outputs, a down count from 15 to 0 results.

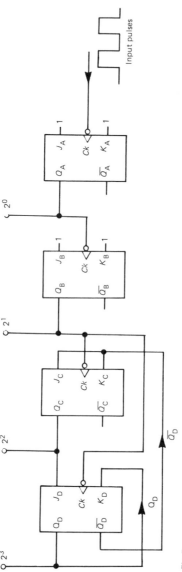

Fig 5

Table 1

INPUT PULSE No.	1 Q_D	2 Q_C	3 Q_B	4 Q_A	5 $\overline{Q}_D$	6 $\overline{Q}_C$	7 $\overline{Q}_B$	8 $\overline{Q}_A$
0	0	0	0	0	1	1	1	1
1	0	0	0	1	1	1	1	0
2	0	0	1	0	1	1	0	1
3	0	0	1	1	1	1	0	0
4	0	1	0	0	1	0	1	1
5	0	1	0	1	1	0	1	0
6	0	1	1	0	1	0	0	1
7	0	1	1	1	1	0	0	0
8	1	0	0	0	0	1	1	1
9	1	0	0	1	0	1	1	0
10	1	0	1	0	0	1	0	1
11	1	0	1	1	0	1	0	0
12	1	1	0	0	0	0	1	1
13	1	1	0	1	0	0	1	0
14	1	1	1	0	0	0	0	1
15	1	1	1	1	0	0	0	0
16	0	0	0	0	1	1	1	1

UP COUNT   DOWN COUNT

6   In digital systems, it is frequently necessary to count up to a number which is not an exact power of 2, e.g. 5 or 12. A pure binary counter may operate in this manner by applying feedback to its bistables to cause a premature resetting of the counter. Additional logic gates may be necessary to achieve shortening of the count in this manner.

As an example of this technique, consider a counter which counts from 0 to 11 and resets on the 12th input pulse. An asynchronous counter of this type is shown in *Fig 5*. A comparison between this counter and a 0-15 counter may be made by reference to their truth tables (see *Table 2*).

It can be seen from *Table 2* that the Q_A and Q_B outputs of both counters are identical, therefore no changes are necessary to these two stages. Q_C must remain reset from a count of 8 onwards, and this is achieved by connecting J_C and K_C to $\overline{Q}_D$. Thus, for a count of 0-7, $\overline{Q}_D$ is at logical 1 and Q_C changes state when bistable C is clocked by Q_B. From a count of 8 onwards, $\overline{Q}_D$ is at a logical 0 and this prevents Q_C from changing state when bistable C is clocked.

Q_D must be set at a count of 8, and reset on a count of 12. This is achieved

Table 2

INPUT PULSE No.	Q_D	Q_C	Q_B	Q_A	Q_D	Q_C	Q_B	Q_A
0	0	0	0	0	0	0	0	0
1	0	0	0	1	0	0	0	1
2	0	0	1	0	0	0	1	0
3	0	0	1	1	0	0	1	1
4	0	1	0	0	0	1	0	0
5	0	1	0	1	0	1	0	1
6	0	1	1	0	0	1	1	0
7	0	1	1	1	0	1	1	1
8	1	0	0	0	1	0	0	0
9	1	0	0	1	1	0	0	1
10	1	0	1	0	1	0	1	0
11	1	0	1	1	1	0	1	1
12	1	1	0	0	0	0	0	0
13	1	1	0	1	0	0	0	1
14	1	1	1	0	0	0	1	0
15	1	1	1	1	0	0	1	1
16	0	0	0	0	0	1	0	0

8-4-2-1 PURE BINARY COUNTER OUTPUTS

8-4-2-1 MODULO 12 COUNTER OUTPUTS

by connecting J_D to Q_C, K_D to Q_D and clocking bistable D with Q_B. The behaviour of bistable D is shown in *Fig 6*.

7 An alternative method of shortening the count of a binary counter is possible if bistables with a CLEAR input are used. A 0 to 11 counter using bistables of this type is shown in *Fig 7*. A NAND gate is used to detect the arrival of the 12th input pulse, and force all bistables to reset. This is accomplished by detecting the condition when Q_C and Q_D are both at logical 1 (a count of 12) and using the resulting logical 0 output from the NAND gate to reset bistables C and D.

8 Much counting in everyday situations uses a base of 10 (decimal system). Therefore, digital systems which interface with the outside world often need counters which count from 0 to 9, i.e. a **decade counter.** An asynchronous decade counter may be constructed as shown in *Fig 8*. If bistables with a CLEAR input are used, the circuit shown in *Fig 9* may be used.

9 Counter devices and circuits using both TTL and CMOS construction are

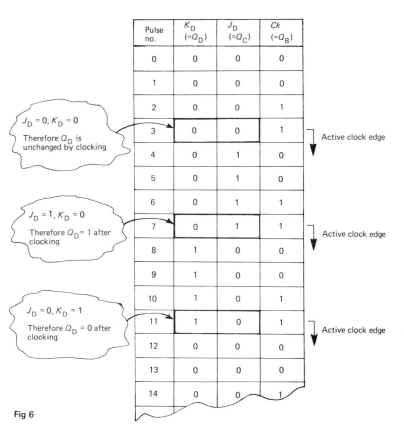

Fig 6

available. In general, TTL circuits operate at higher speed than their CMOS equivalents. A TTL counter may be clocked at frequencies up to 36 MHz. The maximum speed of clocking a CMOS counter depends upon the supply voltage used (V_{DD}). Typical maximum clocking frequencies for CMOS counters are:
(a) 5 MHz (V_{DD} = 5 V)
(b) 10 MHz (V_{DD} = 10 V)

10 CMOS construction is more compact than TTL, therefore a CMOS counter IC normally has many more stages than a TTL counter. A comparison between typical TTL and CMOS counters may be made by referring to *Fig 10*. From this it can be seen that TTL counters seldom have more than four stages, and all outputs are available, but the large number of stages in CMOS counters prevent all outputs from being available due to a limitation on the number of pins on an IC package. The fact that outputs from certain stages are unavailable in CMOS counters may limit their usefulness. CMOS counters are available with up to 21 stages (4045 A) or 24 stages (4521 B). A typical application for the 4045 A counter is that of generating 1 second pulses for digital clock applications (see *Fig 11*).

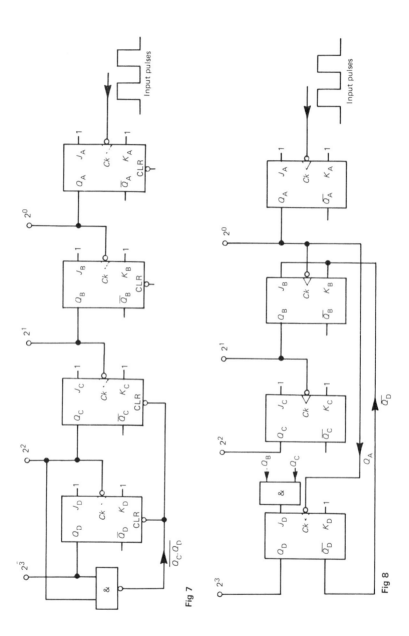

Fig 7

Fig 8

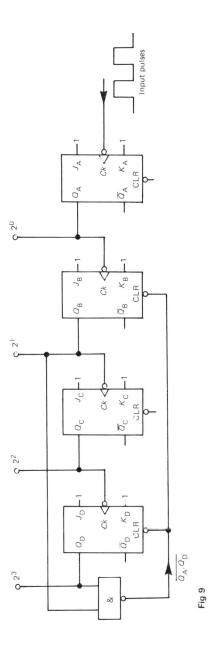

Fig 9

TTL COUNTERS

CMOS COUNTERS

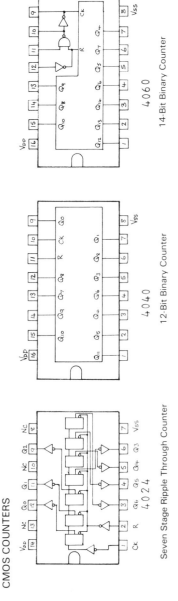

Fig 10

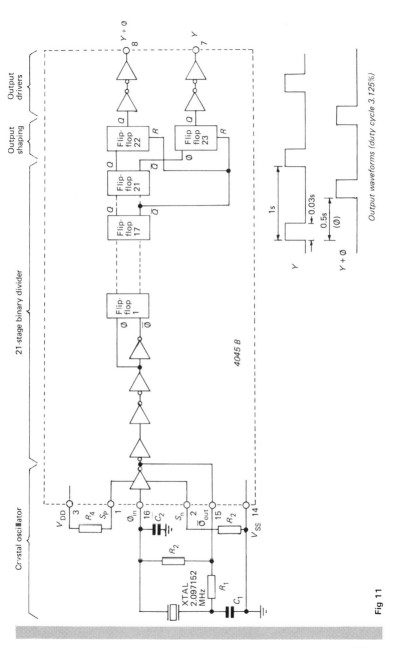

Fig 11

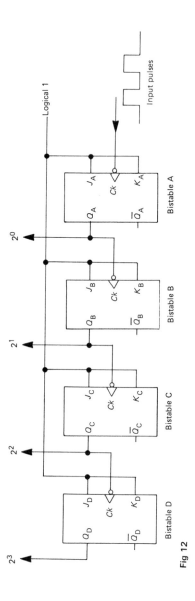

Fig 12

B. WORKED PROBLEMS ON COUNTERS

Problem 1 (a) Draw the logic block diagram of a 4 bit asynchronous 8-4-2-1 pure binary up counter.
(b) Draw timing diagrams for the counter in (a) to show the relationship between input pulses, Q_A, Q_B, Q_C and Q_D for a count of 0 to 15.
(c) With the aid of the timing diagram in (b), explain the operation of an asynchronous counter.

(a) See *Fig 12* (page 106).
(b) See *Fig 13* (page 108).
(c) Most asynchronous counters use negative edge triggered bistables, and these active edges are indicated on all waveforms in *Fig 13*. Assuming the counter indicates 0000 initially (all bistables reset), the behaviour of the counter in response to input pulses may be summarised as follows:
1st input pulse The active edge of this pulse causes Q_A to change to a logical 1, and the counter indicates 0001 (i.e. 1_{10}).
2nd input pulse The active edge of this pulse causes Q_A to change back to a logical 0, and this causes Q_A to present an active clock edge to bistable B. Therefore, Q_B changes to a logical 1 and the counter indicates 0010 (i.e. 2_{10})
3rd input pulse The active edge of this pulse causes Q_A to change to a logical 1, and the counter indicates 0011 (i.e. 3_{10}).
4th input pulse The active edge of this pulse causes Q_A to change back to a logical 0, and this causes Q_A to present an active clock edge to bistable B. Therefore Q_B changes back to a logical 0, and this causes Q_B to present an active edge to bistable C. Therefore Q_C changes to a logical 1 and the counter indicates 0100 (i.e. 4_{10})

Counting progresses in the manner described, each bistable being clocked when the output of the previous stage presents it with an active clock edge.

Problem 2 With the aid of a diagram, explain what is meant by the term **'transitional counts'** or **'dynamic hazards'** in relation to asynchronous counters.

In electronic circuits there is a short time delay between the application of an input signal change and the response of the output to this change (see *Fig 14*). This delay is known as a **'propogation delay'** and is caused by the effects of capacitance, transition times and storage effects. In an asynchronous counter, propogation delays are accumulative, and lead to the production of out-of-sequence counts, known as **'transitional counts'**. For example, the effect of changing from a count of 7 to a count of 8 in an asynchronous counter is shown in *Fig 15*.

It can be seen from *Fig 15* that between a count of 7 and 8, transitional counts of 6, 4 and 0 are produced. The number of transitional counts, and therefore, the time taken for the count to stabilize, is determined by the

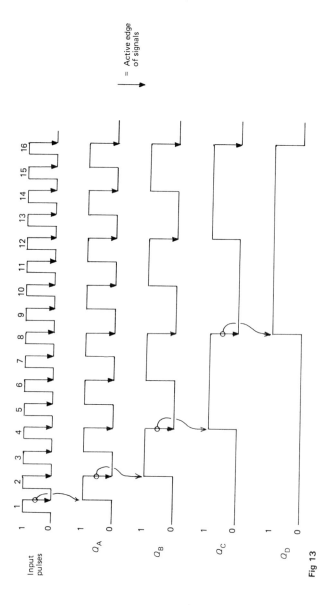

Fig 13

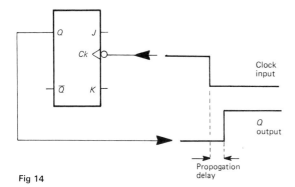

Fig 14

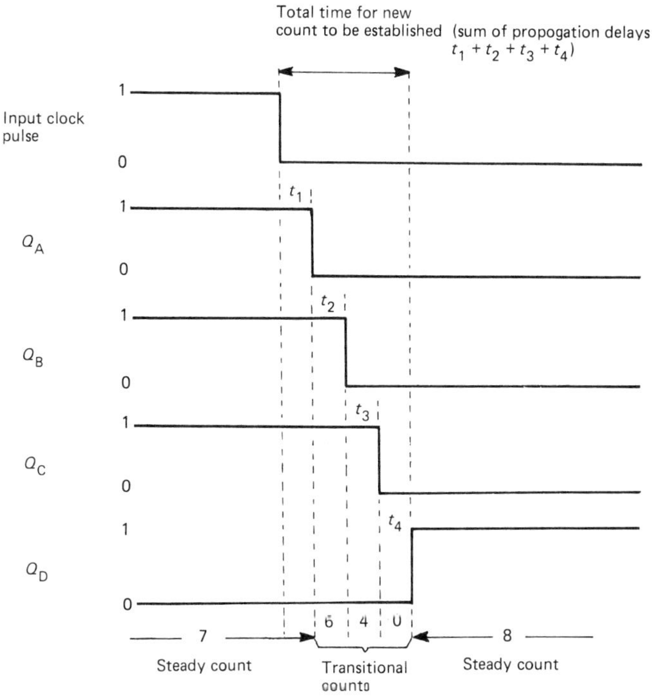

Fig 15

number of bistables which must change state to establish the next count. It can be seen that the worst condition occurs when **all** bistables in a counter change state, and this limits the maximum clocking frequency.

Problem 3 (a) Explain the use of the term **'modulo'** in connection with binary counters.
(b) Draw the logic block diagram of a variable modulo counter and explain its action.

(a) The modulo of a counter refers to the number of distinct counting states that a counter passes through before repeating. Thus, a counter which has 16 different counting states (0 to 15), is called a **'modulo 16'** counter; a decade counter (0 to 9) is called a **'modulo 10'** counter. In some counters the number of different counting states is variable and these counters are known as **'modulo n'** (or $\div n$) counters.

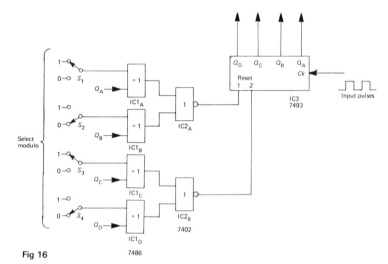

Fig 16

(b) See *Fig 16*. ICs 1 and 2 form a logic comparator circuit. The required modulo is set up in binary form on switches S1-S4, and when the counter outputs match the settings of S1-S4, all outputs of IC1 become logical 0. Therefore IC2 outputs both become logical 1, which resets the counter.

Problem 4 Draw the logic block diagram of a synchronous decade counter and explain how it achieves the correct counting sequence.

Operation of the synchronous decade counter illustrated in *Fig 17* may be summarised as follows:
Counter stage A: Q_A must change state every time the counter is clocked by an input pulse. This is achieved by connecting both J_A and K_A to logical 1.
Counter stage B: Q_B must change state on every second clock input pulse up to

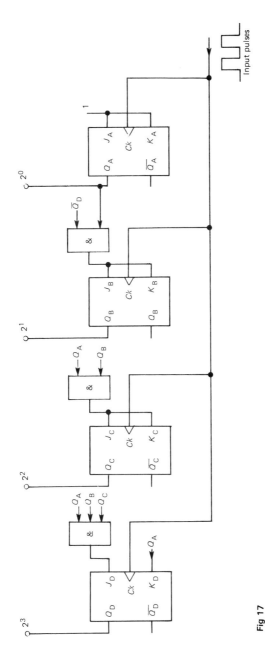

Fig 17

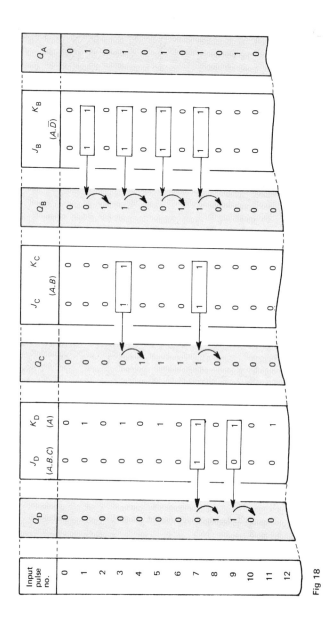

Fig 18

a count of 8, but then remain at logical 0 for 4 clock periods. This is achieved by connecting both J_B and K_B to Q_A, but gating Q_A with $\bar{Q}_D$ (AND gate) to prevent Q_B from changing state upon arrival of the 10th clock input pulse.

Counter stage C: Q_C must change to logical 1 upon arrival of the 4th pulse in the counting sequence, and change back on the 8th pulse. Prior to the arrival of each of these pulses, both Q_A and Q_B are at logical 1. This condition may be detected by ANDing Q_A and Q_B and using the resultant output to precondition J_C and K_C.

Counter stage D: Q_D must be at logical 1 for counts of 8 and 9 in sequence, and logical 0 for all other values. This is achieved by connecting K_D to Q_A and J_D to the output of an AND gate with Q_A, Q_B and Q_C as its inputs. At a count of 7, Q_A, Q_B and Q_C are all logical 1, thus J_D and K_D are both at logical 1 and Q_D changes state upon arrival of the next clock pulse. At a count of 9, K_D is at logical 1 (since $Q_A = 1$) and J_D is at logical 0, and the next clock pulse causes Q_D to return to logical 0.

The states of Q, J and K for each stage during a counting sequence are shown in *Fig 18*.

Problem 5 Show how a 7490 decade counter may be connected to give (a) an asymmetrical ÷ 10, and (b) a symmetrical ÷ 10.

Draw timing diagrams to show the states of all outputs during a full counting sequence.

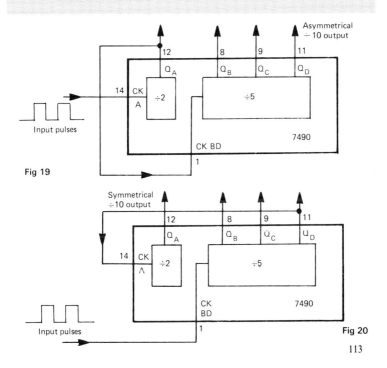

Fig 19

Fig 20

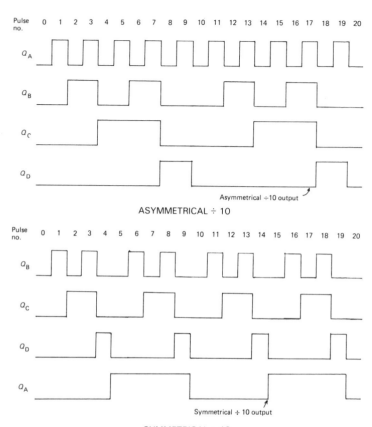

Fig 21

A 7490 decade counter consists of a ÷2 section (A) and a ÷5 section (BD) which may be connected in cascade. An asymmetrical ÷10 is obtained by using the ÷2 section in front of the ÷5 section, as shown in *Fig 19*. A symmetrical ÷10 is obtained by connecting the ÷2 section after the ÷5 section. This arrangement is shown in *Fig 20*, and is known as a **bi-quinary counter.**

Timing diagrams for both types of counter are shown in *Fig 21*. The difference between asymmetrical and symmetrical ÷10 outputs is clearly shown.

Problem 6 (a) Explain how a 4-stage asynchronous counter may be operated as an 8-4-2-1 pure binary down counter.
(b) Draw the logic block diagram of a 4-stage pure binary up/down asynchronous counter and briefly explain its operation.

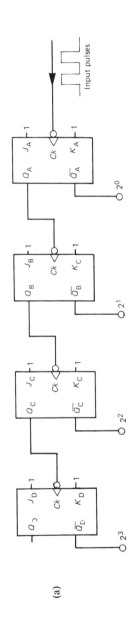
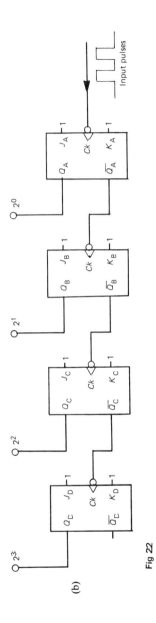

Fig 22

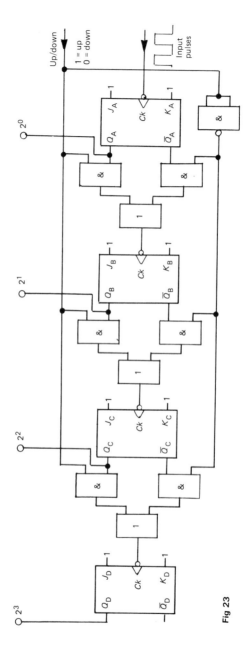

Fig 23

(a) Two methods are available to create a down count in an asynchronous binary counter. These are:
(i) clock each stage from Q of the previous stage and use $\overline{Q}$ of each stage as the counter outputs (see *Fig 22(a)*), and (ii) clock each stage from $\overline{Q}$ of the previous stage and use Q of each stage as the counter outputs (see *Fig 22(b)*).

(b) An asynchronous counter may be operated as an up/down counter by using extra logic gates to select either Q or $\overline{Q}$ of each stage as the clocking signal for the following stage. A typical 4-stage asynchronous pure binary up/down counter is illustrated in *Fig 23*.

Problem 7 (a) With the aid of diagrams, explain the operation of a 'presettable' counter.
(b) Give an example of the use of such a counter.

(a) A typical presettable counter is illustrated in *Fig 24*. From this it can be seen that, in addition to the normal inputs and outputs associated with a binary counter, a presettable counter also has the following inputs:
(i) Load input; and
(ii) A, B, C and D preset inputs.

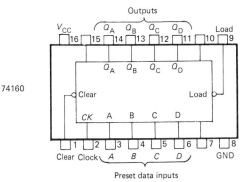

Fig 24

The 'load' input behaves in a similar manner to a 'clear' input, except that instead of causing Q_A, Q_B, Q_C and Q_D to return to zero, they are returned to states preset by inputs A, B, C and D. This behaviour may be observed by studying the timing diagrams shown in *Fig 25*. In this example, D, C, B and A are set to 0011. Therefore, at any point in the counting sequence, if the 'load' input is taken to logical 0, Q_D, Q_C, Q_A and Q_A become 0011 respectively, and further counting continues from this value.

(b) One simple example of the use of a presettable counter is in the 'hours' counter of a 12 hour digital clock. A counter for this purpose must be incremented by 1 until a count of 12 is reached, and then the next input pulse must cause the counter to preset to a count of 1 (not zero). An example of a presettable counter connected to achieve this operation is shown in *Fig 26*.

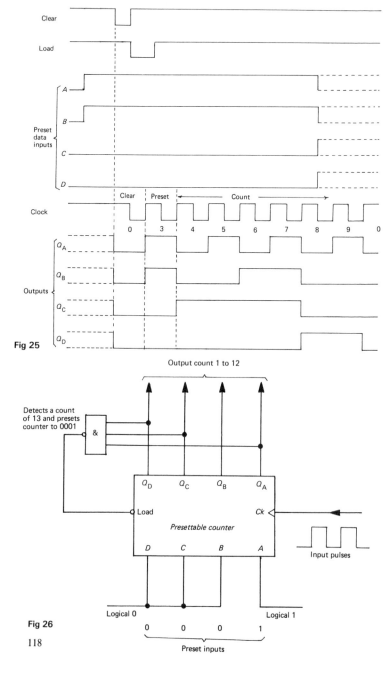

Fig 25

Output count 1 to 12

Fig 26

118

Problem 8 With the aid of a suitable logic block diagram, show how binary counter circuits may be used to construct an event timer, i.e. a digital stopwatch, to indicate 0-99 seconds.

A suitable circuit for a 0-99 second event timer is shown in *Fig 27*. Cascaded decade counters IC_1 and IC_2 are used to count pulses from a 1 Hz oscillator. IC_2 counts up at 1 second intervals, and after 10 input pulses, is reset and

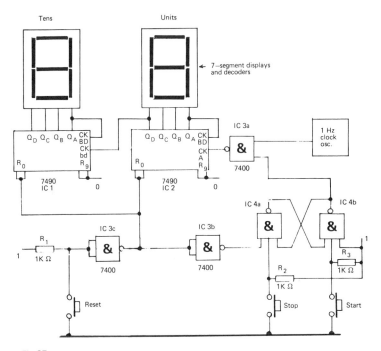

Fig 27

causes IC_1 to be incremented. Binary coded decimal (BCD) outputs from IC_1 and IC_2 are decoded and used to drive 7-segment displays to give a decimal read-out. IC_{4a} and IC_{4b} form an *S-R* bistable which is controlled by START and STOP switches. The output from IC_{4b} is gated with the 1 Hz pulses in IC_{3a} and is used to control starting and stopping of the counters.

Reset inputs of IC_1 and IC_2 (R_o) are controlled by the output of IC_{3c}, and when the RESET switch is closed, IC_{3c} output becomes logical 1, and resets the counters to zero. Also, IC_{3c} output (after inversion by IC_{3b}) is connected to one input of IC_{4a} to ensure that after reset the timer is in the STOP condition.

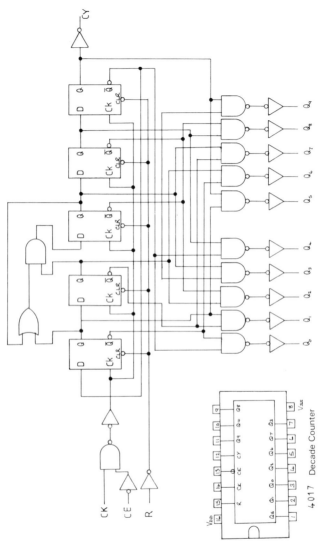

Fig 28

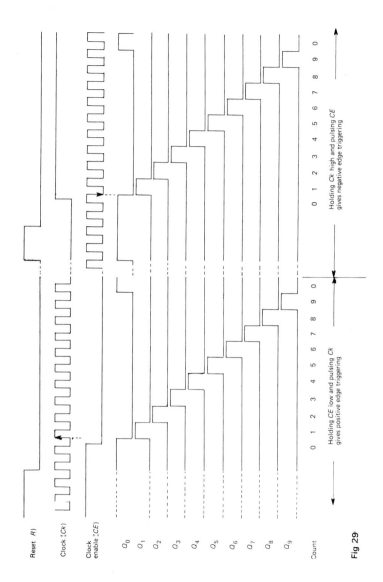

Fig 29

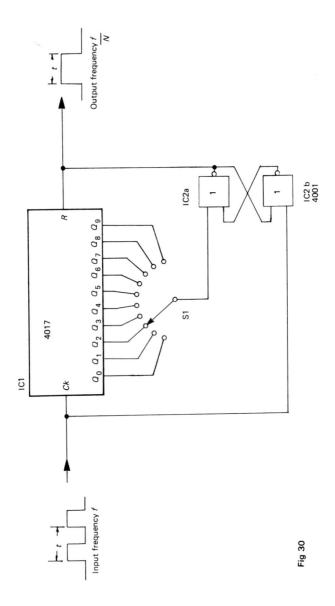

Fig 30

Problem 9 (a) With the aid of diagrams, explain the operation of a 4017 CMOS decade counter, and
(b) Show how a 4017 counter may be operated as a ÷ N counter.

(a) A 4017 CMOS decade counter is a 5-stage **Johnson** or **'twisted ring'** counter, and its internal construction is shown in *Fig 28*. Unlike an 8-4-2-1 BCD counter, this counter has ten separate decoded outputs, Q_0-Q_9, which become logical 1, one at a time, in sequence, as the count proceeds, i.e. decimal rather than BCD outputs. The action of this type of counter is illustrated by the timing diagrams shown in *Fig 29*.

The *CE* input may be used to enable (or inhibit) the clock (*Ck*) input. Used in this manner, a logical 0 on *CE* allows the counter to respond to the positive going edges of the signal applied to *Ck*. Alternatively, *Ck* may be held at logical 1, in which case the counter responds to the negative going edges of a signal applied to *CE*.

(b) Since all outputs of a 4017 counter are decoded, i.e. a logical 1 on each of its outputs corresponds to a particular stage in the counting sequence, shortening the count may be achieved by connecting the appropriate output to the counter reset pin. By using a switch to select any output to cause a reset to take place, a ÷N counter may be constructed. Output pulses may be taken from the reset line, but these are very narrow pulses whose width is determined by the propogation delays in the counter. This is because the condition causing a reset is immediately removed once resetting of the counter occurs. The output pulses may be widened by the use of an *S-R* bistable as shown in *Fig 30*.

The required division ratio is determined by selecting the appropriate Q output by means of switch S1. This signal is used to set the *S-R* bistable formed by IC_{2a} and IC_{2b}, and IC_{2a} output is used to reset counter IC_1. The *S-R* bistable remains set until a logical 1 is applied to IC_{2b} by the leading edge of the next clock pulse. Thus output pulses of width equal to the periodic time of the input signal are obtained.

C FURTHER PROBLEMS ON COUNTERS

(a) SHORT ANSWER PROBLEMS

1 The number of distinct counting states that a counter goes through before repeating is known as its . . . . . .

2 A binary counter in which all bistables change state simultaneously is called a . . . . . . counter.

3 A binary counter in which the bistables change state one after another is called a . . . . . . counter.

4 If the $\overline{Q}$ outputs of a binary counter are selected instead of its Q outputs, a . . . . . . counter is formed.

5 A binary counter which counts from 0 to 9 then back to 0 again is known as a . . . . . . counter.

6 One advantage of a TTL counter compared with a CMOS counter is that it ......

7 One advantage of a CMOS counter compared with a TTL counter is that it ......

8 For high speed counting, a .... counter is required.

9 Propogation delays in a serial counter cause ...... to occur.

10 A binary counter which has all its bistable clock inputs connected in parallel is known as a ...... counter.

11 In order to count from 3 to 15 and back to 3 again, a ...... counter is required.

12 Most serial counters are constructed from bistables which respond to the ...... edge of their clock input pulses.

(b) CONVENTIONAL PROBLEMS

1 Draw the logic block diagram of an asynchronous ÷ 14 binary counter using *J-K* bistables, and explain how the desired counting sequence is obtained.

2 Draw the logic block diagram of a synchronous ÷ 14 binary counter using *J-K* bistables, and explain how the desired counting sequence is obtained.

3 A triangular wave generator makes use of a 4-stage pure binary counter which is made to count up from 0 to 15 and down to 0 repeatedly. Using a binary counter of your choice, draw a logic block diagram to show how the correct counter operation is achieved.

4 A timebase for calibrating an oscilloscope requires output signals at frequencies of 250 kHz, 50 kHz and 1 kHz, draw a logic block diagram of the divider stages necessary to produce these output signals. State suitable IC types for the divider circuits.

6 Registers

A MAIN POINTS CONCERNED WITH REGISTERS

1. It is often necessary in digital circuits to provide temporary storage in which data may be held whilst it is being processed. The basic storage element used for this purpose is the bistable circuit, and when the data being processed consists of a group of bits, a suitable group of interconnected bistables are necessary. Such a group of bistables are known collectively as a **'register'**.
2. Registers may operate in serial or parallel modes. In the serial mode of operation, the data bits of a binary word enter or leave a register in sequence, one bit at a time, in step with the system clock pulses. In the parallel mode of operation, all data bits of a binary word enter or leave a register simultaneously, in step with a single pulse from the system clock.
3. Four basic register types are possible, and these are:
   (a) serial input to serial output (SISO);
   (b) serial input to parallel output (SIPO);
   (c) parallel input to serial output (PISO); and
   (d) parallel input to parallel output (PIPO) (buffer register).
   A register commonly used to perform serial data movements is known as a **'shift register'**.
4. The logic block diagram of a typical serial input/parallel output shift register is shown in *Fig 1*. This circuit behaves as follows.
   Prior to clocking, the J and K inputs of each bistable are previous stage in the register, except for the first stage, whose J and K inputs are determined by the serial input data. The effect of this arrangement is for clocking to cause each stage to adopt the state of the previous stage in the register, except for the first stage which is set or reset according to the serial input data. Therefore, each clock pulse causes data already in the register to be shifted one place to the left, and each new bit of serial input data to be clocked into the first stage. Data in the last stage is clocked out and lost. After four clock pulses, four bits of serial data are clocked into the shift register and are available as parallel outputs from Q_A to Q_D. This action is shown in *Fig 2* for a four bit serial input data stream of 1101.

B WORKED PROBLEMS ON REGISTERS

Problem 1 (a) Draw a simple block diagram of a 4-bit register showing: (i) serial input; (ii) parallel inputs; (iii) serial output; (iv) parallel outputs; and (v) clock and load inputs.
(b) Briefly explain how this register may be used to convert parallel data 1010 into serial form.

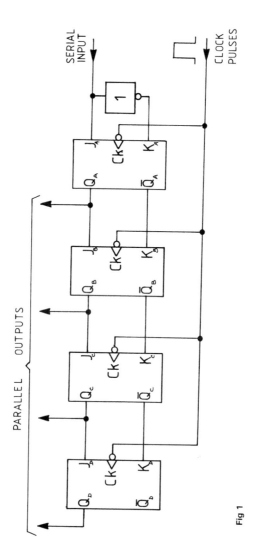

Fig 1

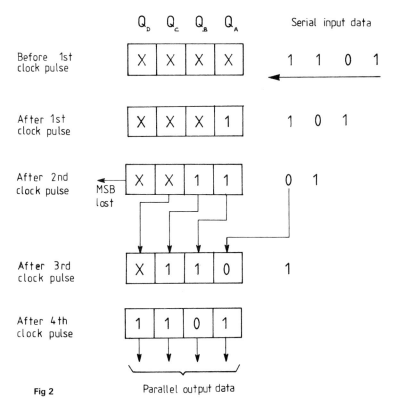

Fig 2

(a) See *Fig. 3*.
(b) Parallel data 1010 may be converted into serial form by the following process:
 (i) apply 1010 to parallel inputs E, F, G and H;
 (ii) apply a load pulse to the load input (*Ld*);
 (iii) apply clock pulses to the clock input (*Ck*) to clock out serial data from the serial output terminal (*So*).
 A complemented ($\overline{So}$) serial output is also available.

Problem 2 Draw the logic block diagram of a 4 stage, serial in/parallel out shift registered constructed from: (a) clocked R-S bistables; (b) D-type bistables.

(a) See *Fig. 4*.
(b) See *Fig. 5*.

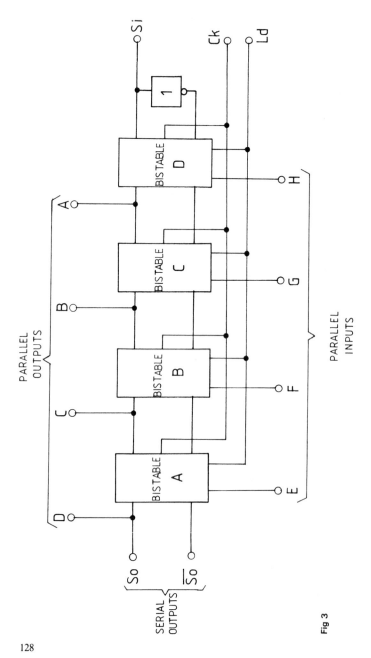

Fig 3

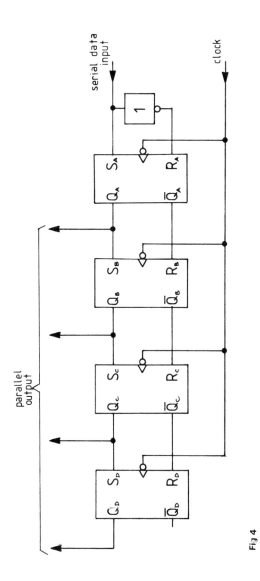

Fig 4

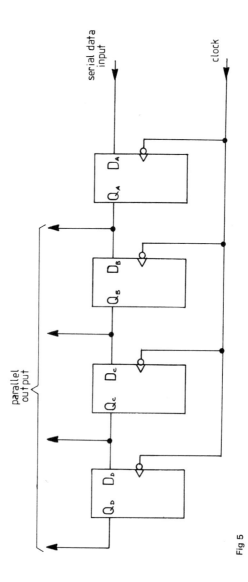

Fig 5

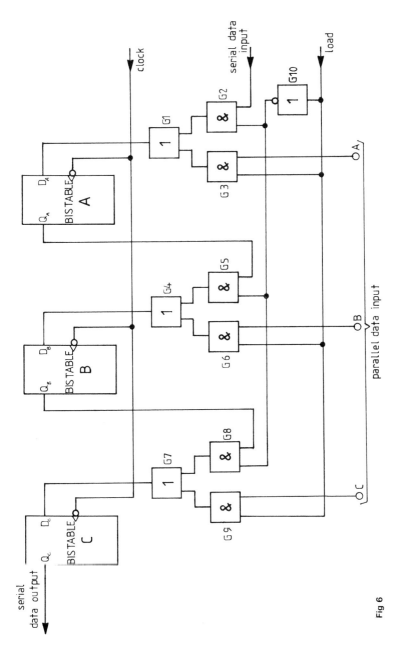

Fig 6

Problem 3 With the aid of a logic block diagram, show how a 3-stage shift register may be loaded with parallel data.

The logic block diagram of a 3-stage shift register with parallel loading facility is shown in *Fig 6*. Logic gates G_1 to G_{10} provide gating for the input of each stage such that each D terminal may be connected to either Q of the previous stage (serial data input in the case of the first stage only), or to the parallel data inputs A, B and C.

The logic state of the 'load' terminal determines the source of data for each stage and its action may be studied by considering the operation of stage B. If the 'load' terminal is at logical 0, one input of G_6 is held at logical 0 and its output is therefore also at logical 0. Due to the action of G_{10}, one input of G_5 is held at logical 1, therefore G_5 output is determined by the state of Q_A. The output of G_4, and hence D_B is also determined by the state of Q_A, i.e. D_B is effectively connected to Q_A under these conditions. If the 'load' terminal is at logical 1, G_{10} output applies a logical 0 to one input of G_5 and its output is therefore held at logical 0, irrespective of the state of Q_A. One input of G_6 is held at logical 1 by the 'load' input, and the output of G_6 is therefore determined by the state of parallel input line B. The output of G_4 (and hence D_B) is also determined by the state of parallel input line B, and this logic state is clocked into bistable B upon arrival of the next clock pulse.

Problem 4 Draw the logic block diagram of a 4-stage register with **'shift right'** and **'shift left'** capabilities and describe how it operates.

The logic block diagram of a 4-stage shift register with 'shift right' and 'shift left' capabilities is shown in *Fig 7*. Logic gates G_5 to G_{24} form data selector circuits, which connect each of the bistable D inputs to one of four signal sources. These sources are:
(i) the Q output of its own bistable;
(ii) the Q output of the bistable to its immediate right (or D_{SL} serial data input if bistable A);
(iii) the Q output of the bistable to its immediate left (or D_{SR} serial data input if bistable D);
(iv) a parallel data input line.
This enables one of the following operations to be carried out·
(i) hold data (data in each bistable is not changed by the clocking action);
(ii) shift left data;
(iii) shift right data; and
(iv) parallel load data.
The operation of each of the data selectors may be studied by considering the gating circuit at the input of bistable B, as shown in *Fig 8*.

Mode control inputs S_0 and S_1, which are available in true and complemented form, provide four possible control combinations. Each combination applies a logical 1 to two inputs of one of the three input AND gates G_9 to G_{12}. The remaining three gates have at least one logical 0 applied to one of their inputs, and their outputs are therefore at logical 0. The selected

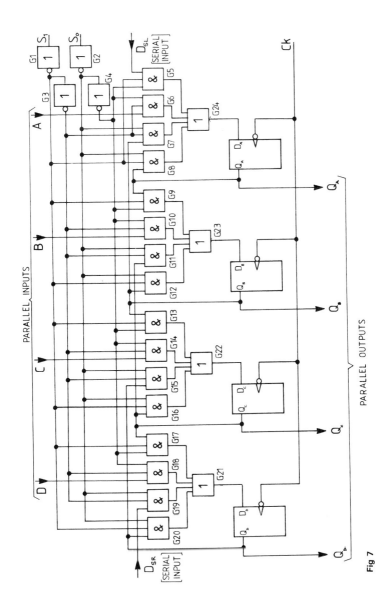

Fig 7

S_1	S_0	OPERATION
0	0	hold
0	1	shift left
1	0	shift right
1	1	parallel load

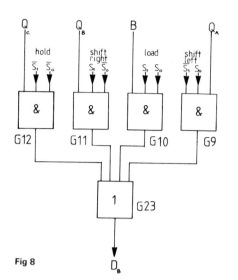

Fig 8

gate, however, has an output whose logic level is determined by the logic state of its third input, i.e. the selected input signal Q_C, Q_B, B or Q_A. The outputs of G_9 to G_{12} are combined in OR gate G_{23}, and the output of this gate provides the D input to bistable B.

Problem 5 Explain how a shift register may be used as a **'ring counter'**.

A shift register may be used as a ring counter by connecting the Q and $\overline{Q}$ outputs of the final stage back to its inputs, as shown in *Fig 9*. With this type of register, data is not shifted out to the left and lost, but instead, is shifted back into the register at its right and keeps circulating through the register.

If all of the Q outputs are initially at logical 0, i.e. the register is cleared, then

Fig 9

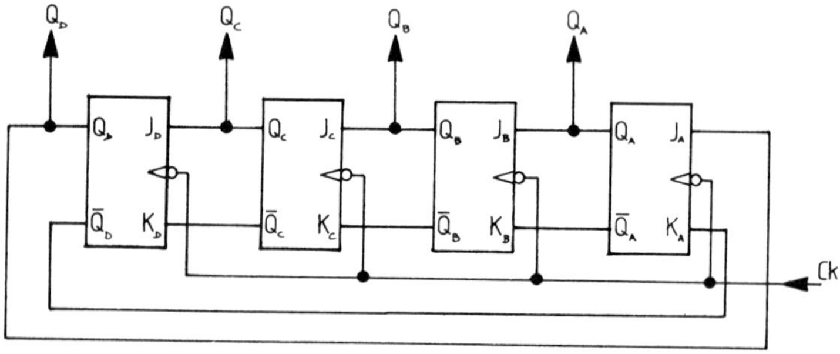

nothing happens when the register is clocked, since all J inputs are at [?]. The counter must first be started by setting Q_A to logical 1, and the count sequence proceeds as shown in *Table 1*. It should be noted that this type of counter does not count in a binary sequence, and requires one bistable for each count in the sequence.

Table 1

Ck pulse no.	Q_D	Q_C	Q_B	Q_A
0	0	0	0	1
1	0	0	1	0
2	0	1	0	0
3	1	0	0	0
4	0	0	0	1

Table 2

Ck pulse no.	Q_D	Q_C	Q_B	Q_A
0	0	0	0	0
1	0	0	0	1
2	0	0	1	1
3	0	1	1	1
4	1	1	1	1
5	1	1	1	0
6	1	1	0	0
7	1	0	0	0
8	0	0	0	0
9	0	0	0	1

Two problems arise with ring counters. The first problem is that a ring counter is not self-starting in its basic state and must have a logical 1 loaded into it before it can count. The second problem is that if further logical 1's are loaded, e.g. due to noise, an invalid count sequence results and a ring counter is unable to get out of this situation. A ring counter does, however, have the advantage of having fully decoded outputs without the need for further logic gates.

A ring counter may be made self-starting by reversing the feedback connections from the final Q and $\bar{Q}$ outputs, and is then known as a **'twisted ring'** counter or **'Johnson'** counter. A counter of this type is shown in *Fig 10*. (See *Worked Problem 9,* chapter 5.)

The count sequence for a twisted ring counter is shown in *Table 2*, and it can be seen from this table that this type of counter has a further advantage in that it has twice as many different output states for the same number of stages when compared with an ordinary ring counter. The outputs of this type of counter require decoding.

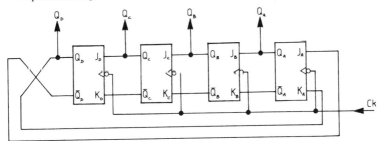

Fig 10

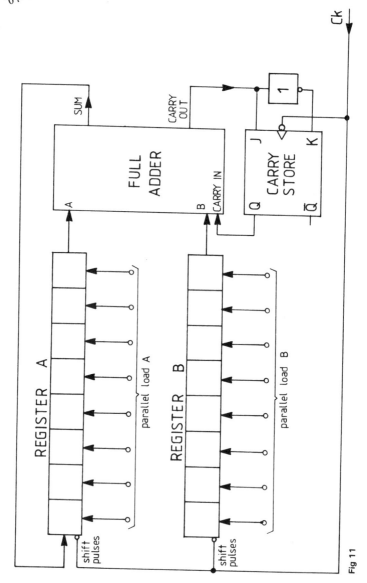

Fig 11

Problem 6 Explain how shift registers may be used in the process of adding two 8-bit binary numbers.

Binary numbers may be added together by using either a parallel or a serial addition process. Addition is accomplished by using a **'full adder'** circuit, and for parallel addition, one full adder is required for each pair of digits to be added, e.g. the addition of two 8-bit binary numbers requires eight full adder circuits to be used. The serial addition process requires only one full adder circuit, and pairs of digits must be shifted in and added in sequence. The logic block diagram of a serial binary adder is shown in *Fig 11*.

The two binary numbers to be added are first parallel loaded into registers A and B. The first two bits in the registers are taken from the serial outputs and applied to the full adder and the resultant sum is fed back to the serial input of register A. Any carry resulting from this addition is applied to the input of a **'carry store'** bistable. Application of the first clock pulse causes the SUM to be clocked in at the serial input to register A, and the **'carry out'** to be clocked into the carry store bistable. All bits in both registers are shifted one place to the right so that the next pair of digits (and any carry from a previous addition) are presented to the full adder. This process is repeated a total of eight times, after which the sum of the two numbers is left in register A and register B is cleared. Register B may, if required, be loaded with a new number which can then be added to the sum in register A by a similar process to that already described, i.e. register A acts as an **'accumulator'**.

Table 3 TTL registers

TTL type No.	No. of stages	Max. clock frequency	Operating modes
7494	4	10 MHz	(i) serial-in, serial-out (ii) dual source, parallel-in, parallel-out (iii) clear
7495	4	36 MHz	(i) left-shift or right-shift (ii) serial-in, serial-out (iii) serial-in, parallel-out (iv) parallel-in, serial-out (v) parallel-in, parallel-out
74164	8	36 MHz	(i) gated serial inputs (A and B) (ii) serial-in, serial-out (iii) serial-in, parallel-out (iv) clear
74165	8	26 MHz	(i) serial-in, serial-out* (ii) parallel-in, serial-out* (iii) clock inhibit* *true and complemented outputs available*

Problem 7 Construct a table to compare typical TTL and CMOS registers in terms of the following properties: (a) number of stages; (b) speed of operation; (c) flexibility of operation.

The characteristics of typical TTL and CMOS registers are shown in *Tables 3* and *4*, from which comparisons between the two types may be made.

Table 4 CMOS registers

TTL type No.	No. of stages	Max. clock frequency	Operating modes
4014	8	5.8 MHz (5 V V_{dd}) 14.7 MHz (10 V V_{dd})	(i) serial-in, serial-out (ii) parallel-in, serial-out (iii) parallel outputs from last three stages only
4015	4 (dual)	8 MHz (5 V V_{dd}) 14 MHz (10 V V_{dd})	(i) serial-in, serial-out (ii) serial-in, parallel-out (iii) clear
4035	4	5 MHz (5 V V_{dd}) 12 MHz (10 V V_{dd})	(i) serial-in, serial-out (ii) serial-in, parallel-out (iii) parallel-in, parallel-out (iv) parallel-in, serial-out (v) clear (vi) selection of true or complemented outputs
40195	4	9 MHz (5 V V_{dd}) 14 MHz (10 V V_{dd})	(i) serial-in, serial-out (ii) serial-in, parallel-out (iii) parallel-in, parallel-out (iv) parallel-in, serial-out (v) shift-right, shift-left, hold & parallel load modes (vi) clear

C FURTHER PROBLEMS ON REGISTERS

(a) SHORT ANSWER PROBLEMS

1 A register consists of a group of ......

2 A register in which all data bits enter or leave in sequence is known as a ......

3 A register in which all data bits enter or leave simultaneously is known as a
   . . . . . .

4 A register which is used to perform serial data movements is known as a
   . . . . . .

5 The binary number stored in a register may be doubled in value by means of a
   . . . . . . operation.

6 The binary number stored in a register may be halved in value by means of a
   . . . . . . operation.

7 A register which has parallel inputs and outputs only is known as a . . . . . .

8 If the outputs of the last stage of a shift register are connected back to the
   inputs of the first stage, a . . . . . . is formed.

9 A typical maximum clocking frequency for a TTL register is . . . . . .

10 A typical maximum clocking frequency for a CMOS register is . . . . . .

(b) CONVENTIONAL PROBLEMS

1 Draw a block diagram of a 4-bit register, showing:
   (a) serial input;
   (b) parallel input;
   (c) parallel output;
   (d) serial output;
   (e) clock input.

2 (a) Explain how serial data 1011 may be loaded into a 4-bit register.
   (b) Explain how parallel data 1010 may be loaded into a 4-bit register and
       shifted out serially.
   Write down the register contents at each relevant stage in the above processes.

3 Name two arithmetic processes in a digital system which need the use of a shift
   register, and explain how the register is used for each of the two named
   processes.

7 Digital storage devices

A MAIN POINTS CONCERNED WITH DIGITAL STORAGE DEVICES

1   The basic requirements for all digital storages are:
    (a) a number of individual storage elements known as **'memory cells'**, each capable of temporary or permanent storage of a single binary digit;
    (b) a system of addressing which provides a means of selecting a specified memory cell (or group of cells) within the memory device;
    (see *Problems 2 and 3*)
    (c) a method of storing data in specified locations; and
    (d) a method of reading data from specified locations.
2   Memory circuits used in digital systems may be classified as:
    (a) **volatile;** or
    (b) **non-volatile.**
    A volatile memory loses its stored data if its power supply is not continuously maintained. A non-volatile memory retains its stored data permanently, and removal of its power supply does not result in the loss of its stored data.
3   The following six types of memory devices are commonly found in digital systems:
    (a) **Random access memory (RAM)**
    This is a type of memory in which any particular storage location (address) may be directly selected without first having to sequence through other locations, i.e. one storage location may be accessed as easily as any other regardless of its physical position within the particular memory device. Any type of memory may employ random access of data, although the term 'RAM' has become generally accepted (incorrectly) to mean **'read-write'** memory, i.e. memory in which the user may either read or write to specified locations whilst in its normal circuit environment.
       Two different types of semiconductor read-write memory are used in digital systems, and both types are volatile. These are
    (i) **Static RAM** in which bistable or flip-flop circuits are used as storage elements. With this type of memory, the stored data is retained permanently provided its power supply is continuously maintained; and
    (ii) **Dynamic RAM (DRAM)** in which capacitors are used as temporary storage elements. Information is stored as a charge or non-charge on a capacitor, but leakage effects cause loss of charge and hence loss of stored information. Therefore the charges on these capacitors must be restored at frequent intervals (≈ 2 ms) to prevent loss of stored information, and this process is known as **'refreshing'**.
    (See *Problems 1 and 4 to 8.*)
    (b) **Read-only memory (ROM)**
    This is a non-volatile memory, used for the storage of permanent unalterable

data. Data are stored in ROM during the final metallizing stage of manufacture, by means of a mask programming process, using a mask constructed according to information supplied by the customer. The construction of a mask is an expensive process, hence ROMs are only used in high volume applications.
(See *Problems 9 and 10.*)

(c) **Programmable read-only memory (PROM)**
A PROM fulfils basically the same functions as a ROM except that whereas a ROM must be programmed by its manufacturers, a PROM is programmed by its user, i.e. it is **'field programmable'**. A PROM device is supplied by its manufacturer in a blank state with all bits held at logical 0 or logical 1, by means of small fusible links. Programming a PROM involves its user blowing (or fusing) links in selected locations, thus changing the logic level in these locations. Like a ROM, once programmed a PROM cannot be reprogrammed.
(See *Problem 11.*)

(d) **Erasable programmable read-only memory (EPROM)**
An EPROM also fulfills basically the same functions as a ROM, and like a PROM, it is also field programmable. Its main advantage, however, is that it may be erased and reprogrammed. An EPROM uses floating gate avalanche (FAMOS) technology, and is supplied in its blank state by its manufacturer, with all locations at logical 0 or logical 1. Programming an EPROM involves storing electrical charges on selected FET floating gates to change these particular locations to the opposite logic state. Erasure of an EPROM (changing all locations to the same logic state) is achieved by exposing the entire memory chip to ultraviolet light.

The main disadvantages of an EPROM are:
(i) selected locations cannot be erased, which means that the entire memory must be erased and reprogrammed if changes are required in only one or two locations; and
(ii) the method of erasure prevents this type of memory from being reprogrammed in circuit.
(See *Problems 12 and 13.*)

(e) **Electrically alterable read-only memory (EAROM)**
An EAROM performs the same basic functions as ROM, PROM and EPROM devices, but its stored data may be changed electrically by the application of suitable control signals. It is therefore sometimes called a **'read mostly'** memory. Erasure of an EAROM is carried out electrically by manipulation of its control inputs and voltages, but, unlike an EPROM, and EAROM may have selected blocks or individual locations erased without having to erase the entire memory. Since an EAROM is erased electrically, it is possible to arrange for reprogramming to take place without removal from its normal circuit environment. (See *Problems 14 and 15.*)

(f) **Ferrite core store.**
This is a non-volatile read-write memory which uses residual magnetism in small rings of magnetic material (ferrite cores) to store digital information. The direction of the magnetic field in a ferrite core determines whether a logical 0 or a logical 1 is stored. This type of memory is very expensive to manufacture and has been largely superceded by semiconductor memory.
(See *Problems 16 to 18.*)

B WORKED PROBLEMS ON DIGITAL STORAGE DEVICES

Problem 1 Draw a block diagram to illustrate the main sections of a typical 1 K bit static RAM (read/write memory).

A typical 1 K bit static RAM is the type 2102 which uses a 32×32 bit memory array, arranged as shown in *Fig 1*.

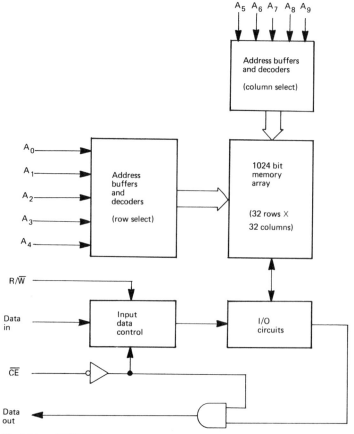

Fig 1 A type 2102 RAM

Problem 2 Explain the term **'addressing'** when used in connection with digital storage devices.

142

Digital storage devices consist of a very large number of individual storage locations. Each storage location contains a **'memory cell'** which is capable of storing a single binary digit (0 or 1). When data is transferred to and from the storage device it is important that:
(a) the desired location can be readily identified; and
(b) only one location is selected at any given time.

Therefore, each location is assigned a unique identifying label called an **'address'**. This takes the form of a unique binary number for each memory cell. Addressing a storage device consists of applying the binary address of the desired location to the address inputs of the storage device. The content of the selected location is then routed to the data output terminal of the storage device.

Problem 3 With the aid of diagrams, explain how memory devices are arranged internally to reduce the number of external address lines.

The number of address lines required for a memory device is reduced by organising the memory cells in the form of a matrix. A further reduction in the number of address lines is obtained by decoding binary address inputs into individual outputs (see *Fig 2*).

The address input lines are divided into two groups which are decoded separately within the memory device to form two sets of memory cell select signals. These are known as **'row select' (X)** and **'column select' (Y)** signals, and they are arranged in the form of a matrix. A memory cell is connected to the X and Y lines at each intersection of the matrix, and is selected when both its X and Y lines are energised (see *Fig 3*).

Using this system, it can be seen that 64 different locations may be addressed by the use of only 6 address inputs. This principle may be used for larger memories; for example, a 32×32 matrix enables 1 K (1024) memory locations to be addressed by the use of only 10 address input lines.

Problem 4 With the aid of a circuit diagram, explain the operation of a memory cell in a typical static RAM (read-write memory).

The circuit diagram of a 2102 memory cell is illustrated in *Fig 4*. This device uses NMOS construction and each memory cell consists of two inverter circuits arranged as a flip flop. TR1 and TR2 are the cross-coupled switching transistors, and TR3 and TR4 are used as active pull up resistors. Transistors TR5, 6, 7 and 8 are controlled by row and column select signals and hence determine when this particular cell is selected. Selection of a particular memory cell takes place as follows:

When column select (Y_0) is activated (logical 1), TR7 and TR8 conduct and connect all cells in this particular column of the memory matrix to the data input/output lines. When row select (X_0) is activated (logical 1), TR5 and TR6 conduct (along with equivalent transistors of all other memory cells in the selected row).

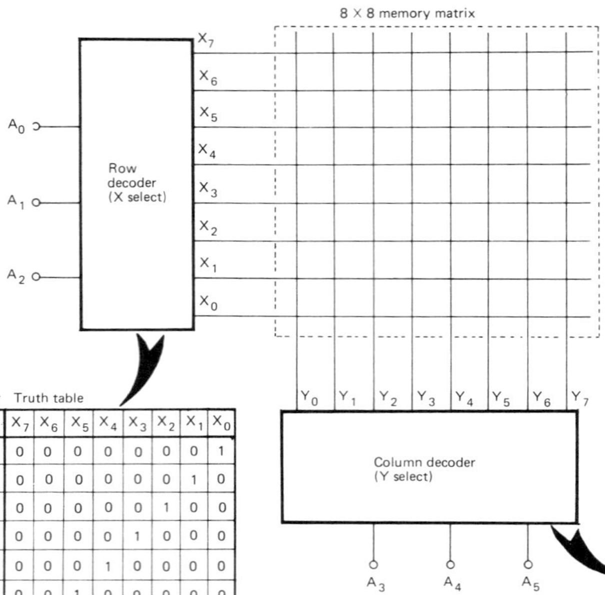

Row decoder Truth table

A_2	A_1	A_0	X_7	X_6	X_5	X_4	X_3	X_2	X_1	X_0
0	0	0	0	0	0	0	0	0	0	1
0	0	1	0	0	0	0	0	0	1	0
0	1	0	0	0	0	0	0	1	0	0
0	1	1	0	0	0	0	1	0	0	0
1	0	0	0	0	0	1	0	0	0	0
1	0	1	0	0	1	0	0	0	0	0
1	1	0	0	1	0	0	0	0	0	0
1	1	1	1	0	0	0	0	0	0	0

Column decoder Truth table

A_5	A_4	A_3	Y_7	Y_6	Y_5	Y_4	Y_3	Y_2	Y_1	Y_0
0	0	0	0	0	0	0	0	0	0	1
0	0	1	0	0	0	0	0	0	1	0
0	1	0	0	0	0	0	0	1	0	0
0	1	1	0	0	0	0	1	0	0	0
1	0	0	0	0	0	1	0	0	0	0
1	0	1	0	0	1	0	0	0	0	0
1	1	0	0	1	0	0	0	0	0	0
1	1	1	1	0	0	0	0	0	0	0

Fig 2

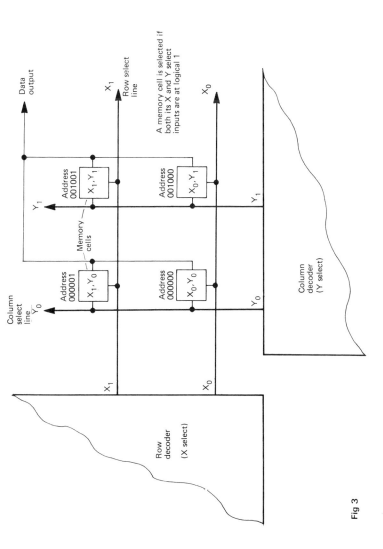

Fig 3

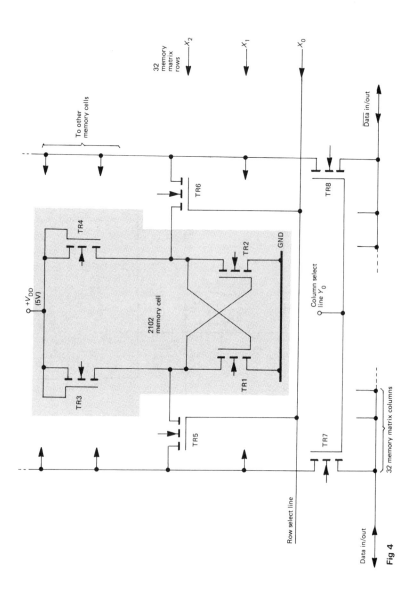

Fig 4

Thus it can be seen that TR5/TR7 and TR6/TR8 effectively behave as AND gates, and only the memory cell which lies at the intersection of the enabled row and column lines is selected. Assuming the memory cell illustrated in *Fig 4* is selected, and the memory is set in the **'write'** mode, data may be stored as follows:

A logical 1 applied to the DATA IN/OUT terminal causes a positive potential to be applied to TR2 gate via TR5 and TR7. This causes TR2 to conduct and its drain potential falls to approximately 0 V, which, in turn, causes TR1 to become non conductive (since its gate is connected to TR2 drain). Thus TR1 drain potential remains at $+V_{DD}$ (logical 1) after the input signal is removed, and a logical 1 is stored on TR1 drain. A logical 0 may be stored by a similar process.

With the RAM switched to the **'read'** mode, data stored at TR1 drain (or its complement at TR2 drain) may be non-destructively interrogated by enabling TR5/7 and TR6/8, i.e. by selecting this particular memory cell.

Problem 5 Draw a block diagram to illustrate the main sections of a typical 4 K bit dynamic RAM (read/write memory).

A typical 4 K bit dynamic RAM is the type 2107 which uses a 64×64 bit memory array, arranged as shown in *Fig 5*.

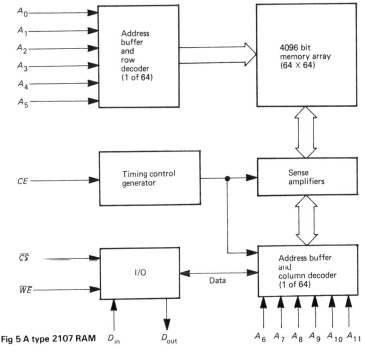

Fig 5 A type 2107 RAM

Problem 6 With the aid of a circuit diagram, explain the operation of a typical dynamic RAM memory cell.

With this type of memory a capacitor is used as the basic storage element and a simplified dynamic memory cell is illustrated in *Fig 6*. The operation of this circuit may be summarised as follows:

(i) **Write data** (S1 closed, S2 open). *C* charges to a voltage level corresponding to the logic level of the input data.

(ii) **Read data** (S1 open, S2 closed). The voltage level on *C* (which represents the stored logic level) is transferred to the output terminal via S2.

A typical one transistor dynamic memory cell is shown in *Fig 7*.

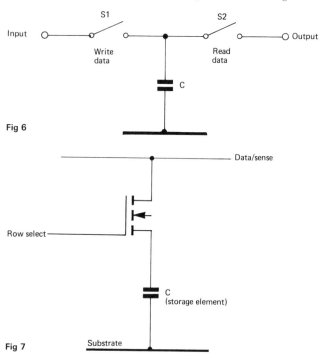

Fig 6

Fig 7

Problem 7 Explain the main advantages and disadvantages of a dynamic RAM compared with a static RAM.

The main advantages of a dynamic RAM compared with a static RAM are:
(i) a dynamic RAM cell is much smaller physically than that of a static RAM,

148

therefore, during manufacture it is possible to use a much greater packing density, i.e. more memory locations on a given chip size.
(ii) A dynamic RAM may consume less power than a static RAM, which is especially important where large amounts of memory are involved, e.g. in computers. The reason for this is that when a dynamic RAM is not being addressed it is in a virtual 'standby' mode with none of its circuits conducting, whereas a static RAM (consisting of thousands of flip flop circuits) must have one transistor in each flip flop conducting at all times so that the stored information may be retained.

*The main **disadvantages** of a dynamic RAM are:*
(i) Due to leakage in its storage capacitors, the information stored in a dynamic RAM is soon lost unless it is repeatedly rewritten into each memory cell at approximately 2 ms intervals of time. This is a process known as **'refreshing'** which requires additional circuitry both internal and external to the dynamic RAM. For this reason, dynamic RAM is unlikely to be used where less than 16 K locations are involved.
(ii) Most dynamic RAMs require multiple supply rails, e.g. $+5V$, $+12V$ and $-5V$, whereas most static RAMs use a single ($+5V$) rail. The multiple voltages may require a more costly power supply unit if these supplies are not already provided for other sections of the circuit.

Problem 8 Explain why 'refreshing' is required in a dynamic RAM and explain how it takes place.

Logical 1's and 0's are stored in a dynamic RAM memory cell as a charge (or no charge) on a capacitor. Leakage paths across this capacitor (particularly during 'read' operations) cause discharging and consequent loss of data to occur. Therefore, memory cells in a dynamic RAM must be 'topped up' at frequent intervals, and this is a process known as **'refreshing'**.

A dynamic RAM is organised internally as shown in *Fig 8,* with one sense amplifier connected to each column of memory cells. Each sense amplifier consists basically of a bistable circuit, connected to the memory cell, and arranged so that it can sense the stored logic level. When a memory cell is read, this bistable latches with its output at logical 0 or logical 1 according to the value it senses, thus connecting the cell storage capacitor to the correct logic level to enable it to be refreshed. Such an arrangement is shown in *Fig 9,* and the action of this sense amplifier is as follows:

$C2$ is charged to approximately $\frac{1}{2}V$ by the precharge circuit.
$C1$ and $C2$ are then simultaneously connected to the sense amplifier which compares the potential across $C1$ with that across $C2$. If the potential of $C1$ is greater than the potential of $C2$, Q becomes a logical 1, thus recharging $C1$ to V volts. If the potential of $C1$ is less than the potential of $C1$, Q becomes a logical 0, thus keeping $C1$ at 0 volts. Clearly, if $C1$ is at logical 1, it must not be allowed to discharge to too low a potential if satisfactory refreshing is to take place.

Refreshing a dynamic RAM, therefore, consists of reading every cell in sequence at time intervals no longer than 2 ms apart. This must be done whether data is required or not (data is usually ignored during refresh cycles anyway). From *Fig 8* it can be seen that selecting a cell in any particular row

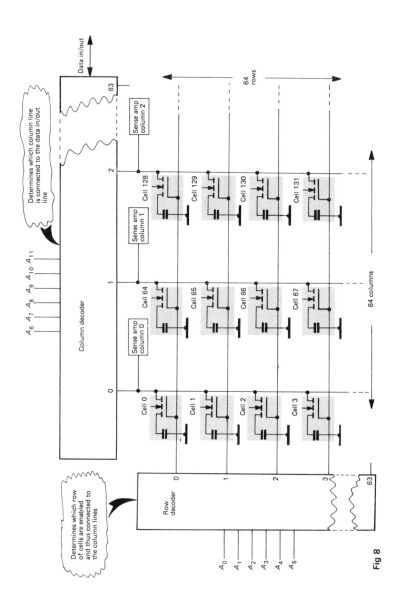

Fig 8

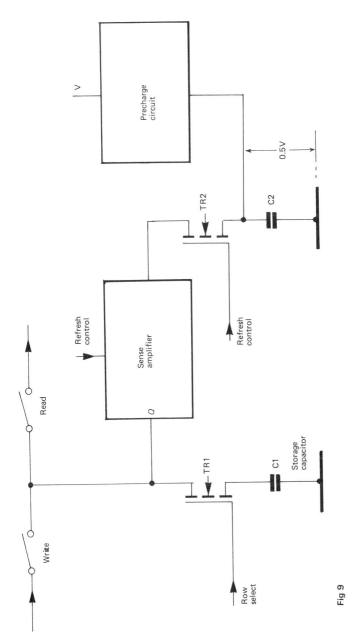

Fig 9

results in all cells in that row being connected to their respective column sense amplifiers. Therefore, a dynamic RAM may be refreshed by simply cycling through all row addresses in sequence.

Problem 9 Draw the block diagram of a typical ROM (read only memory).

A typical ROM is the mask programmable type 2316, 16384 bit (2048 × 8) memory which is illustrated in *Fig 10*.

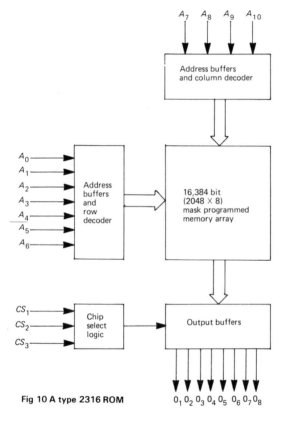

Fig 10 A type 2316 ROM

Problem 10 With the aid of a diagram, explain the principle of operation of a ROM (read only memory) and state typical methods used to store data in a ROM.

152

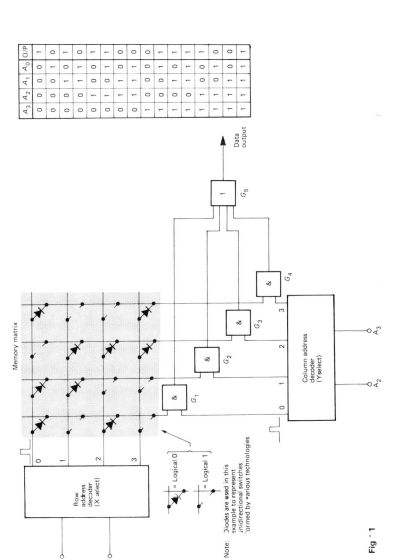

Fig 1

Storage elements for 'read only' memories may be more simple in construction than those necessary for 'read-write' memories. A typical ROM construction is illustrated in *Fig 11* which uses a memory matrix constructed from diodes.

In this circuit, the lower order address lines (A_0/A_1) are decoded to cause a logical 1 to be applied to one of the row lines (X) of the matrix. This causes each of the column lines (Y) to become logical 1 where a diode is fitted, but to remain at logical 0 where no diode is fitted. Each of the column lines is connected to one input of an AND gate (G_1 to G_4).

The higher order address lines (A_2/A_3) are decoded and this causes a logical 1 to be applied to one input of one of the selector AND gates (G_1 to G_4). Thus three of these AND gates have a logical 0 on their output, whilst the fourth gate has a logical 0 or a logical 1, determined by the state of its column line.

Each of the diodes shown in the memory matrix in *Fig 11* represents a unidirectional switch, and the pattern of switches represents the stored information. Various technologies are available for constructing these switches and programming the information into a ROM. These include the following:

(i) **Mask programming** FET or bipolar switches are linked into circuit during the final stages of manufacture of a ROM, using a pattern supplied by the customer. Due to the relatively high cost involved in preparing masks for this process it is only suitable for volume production applications.

(ii) **Fusible link programming** Fuses in series with closed switches (usually bipolar transistors) are provided in all positions of the matrix. Programming information into this type of memory may be carried out by either the manufacturer or the user by blowing fuses in selected locations.

(iii) **Avalanche injection programming** FET switches in a memory matrix are programmed by selectively turning them on by electrical charges induced in their gates by avalanche injection techniques (see *Problem 13*). This process is carried out by the user, and, unlike the previous examples, is reversible for reprogramming purposes.

Problem 11 With reference to a fusible link PROM:
(a) describe the construction and operation of a typical memory cell,
(b) explain how programming is carried out, and
(c) state **three** disadvantages of this type of memory.

(a) Each bit position in this type of memory consists of a transistor switch (bipolar or FET) connected in series with a very small fuse made from nichrome (earlier types), titanium tungsten or polycrystalline silicon. When a PROM is supplied by the manufacturer, all fuses are intact, and all locations are held at the same logic level (0 or 1 according to type). The circuit of a typical bipolar PROM memory cell is shown in *Fig 12*.

This memory cell is selected by applying a logical 1 to its row address line, and as a result, TR1 is biased on (switch closed). If the fuse is intact, a logical 1 is applied to its column select line (from V_{CC} via TR1) and then on to the data output terminal. If the fuse is blown, however, a logical 0 is applied to its column select line despite TR1 being in a conducting state.

(b) A PROM is programmed (usually in special PROM blowing equipment) by carrying out the following sequence of operations:
(i) apply the address of the location to be programmed to the memory address inputs;

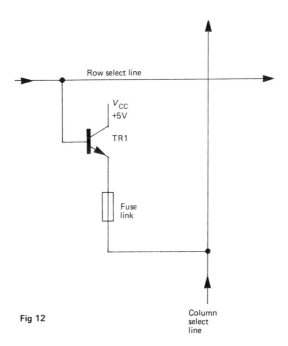

Fig 12

(ii) raise V_{CC} to an elevated programming value (V_{CCP}) of approximately 14 V;
(iii) using the memory data outputs as inputs, apply V_{CCP} to the desired input;
(iv) apply a pulse to the memory chip enable (*CE*) input to actually blow the fuse;
(v) reduce V_{CC} to its normal value (5 V),
(vi) verify that the fuse is actually blown, and repeat (ii) to (v) as necessary;
(vii) wait a given time interval, and repeat (ii) to (vi) for any further bits which are to be programmed at the same address; and
(viii) change the address inputs to that of the next location to be programmed and repeat the procedure described in (ii) to (vii).

(c) Three disadvantages of a PROM are:
(i) they cannot be reprogrammed once used,
(ii) errors cannot be corrected, and
(iii) **'grow back'** may occur in which, after a period of time, blown fuses may remake themselves.

Problem 12 Draw the block diagram of a typical EPROM (erasable programmable read-only memory).

A typical EPROM is the type 2716, 16384 (2048 × 8) memory which is illustrated in *Fig 13*.

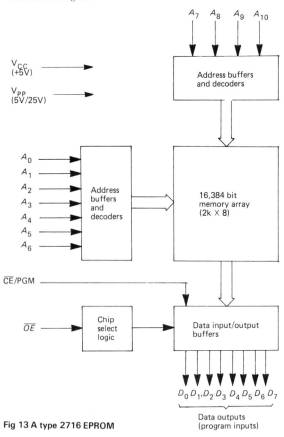

Fig 13 A type 2716 EPROM

Problem 13 With reference to a typical EPROM:
(a) describe the construction and operation of a memory cell,
(b) explain how erasure is accomplished, and
(c) describe the programming procedure.

(a) This type of memory makes use of **floating gate avalanche injection MOS** (FAMOS) technology, and the construction of a typical memory cell is illustrated in *Fig 14*.

EPROMs are supplied by their manufacturer with all locations at the same logic level (0 or 1 according to type). The logic level at any specified

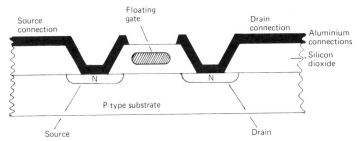

Fig 14

address may be changed by applying a programming potential (V_{PP}) of approximately 25-30 V to the memory cell via the appropriate read/select lines. This potential is applied between drain and source of an FET switch in the memory cell, and causes avalanche breakdown of the drain, with consequent injection of high energy current carriers from the surface of the avalanche region into a floating gate. Since the gate is floating, a charge is accumulated which produces an inversion layer (n-type) at the substrate surface and holds the FET switch in the 'on' state. Once the applied voltage is removed, no path exists for the charge on this gate to leak away and it is retained for a duration of at least ten years. Thus, once an FET switch is programmed in the 'on' state, it remains in that condition.

(b) One of the advantages of an EPROM is that it may be erased and reprogrammed. Erasure is accomplished by exposing the entire memory chip to ultraviolet light (UV) of 2537 angstroms wavelength for a period of 10-20 minutes. A window is provided on each EPROM IC to enable its memory chip to be exposed, see *Fig 15*. The action of the UV light is to effectively overcome the energy barrier and temporarily short circuit the gates to the substrate of all FET switches in the memory.

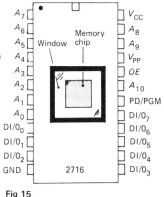

(c) The methods used for programming EPROMs vary considerably from

Fig 15

type to type. As an example, consider the programming sequence used for a 2716 EPROM (see *Fig 13*.):

(i) raise V_{PP} from +5 V to +25 V;
(ii) connect $\overline{OE}$ to logical 1 to disable the outputs;
(iii) apply the address of the location to be programmed to the memory address inputs;
(iv) using the data output pins as inputs, apply data to determine which bits are to be changed to logical 0 and which bits are to remain at logical 1;
(v) apply a 50 ms pulse to the PD/PGM input;
(vi) repeat (iii) to (v) for all other locations to be programmed.

Problem 14 Draw the block diagram of a typical EAROM (electrically alterable read only memory)

A typical EAROM is the type 3400, 4096 bit (1 K × 4) memory which is illustrated in *Fig 16*.

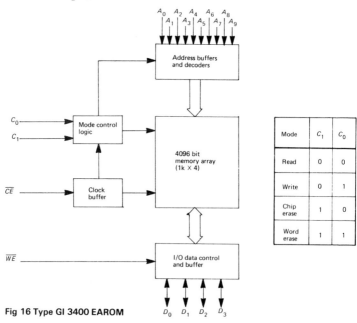

Fig 16 Type GI 3400 EAROM

Problem 15 Describe the construction of an EAROM cell and explain how information is stored.

The gate potential required to switch on a MOSFET (known as its **threshold potential**) is typically 3-4 V, which is too high to allow compatibility with TTL circuits. The threshold of a MOSFET may be reduced by replacing its silicon dioxide insulating layer with **silicon nitride,** but this results in unstable operation with different 'OFF to ON' and 'ON to OFF' thresholds, i.e. a **hysteresis effect.** This hysteresis is caused by charges tunnelling from the substrate into the nitride layer and remaining trapped there.

In most MOSFET memory devices, a thin layer of silicon dioxide is deposited between the substrate and the silicon nitride layer, and this has the effect of stabilizing the threshold potential whilst still maintaining TTL compatibility.

In an EAROM cell, use is made of the hysteresis effect as a means of storing

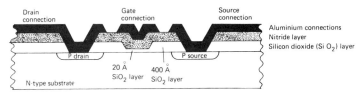

Fig 17

data in a non-volatile manner, and a typical EAROM cell is illustrated in *Fig 17*. In this construction, the silicon dioxide layer is made very thin ($\approx 25\text{Å}$) so that at normal gate potentials charge tunnelling does not occur and TTL compatibility is maintained. If gate potentials of the order -25 V to -30 V are used, however, electrons are driven out of the silicon dioxide/nitride interface and into the substrate material with the result that positive charges are stored in trap sites at the interface. Since silicon dioxide and silicon nitride are both good insulators, the trapped charges are retained for up to ten years.

A trapped positive charge has the same effect as a positive gate bias on a MOSFET and holds the transistor in a low conduction (off) state. This positive charge must also be overcome by externally applied negative gate signals with the result that the switching threshold is raised to approximately -12 V.

An EAROM cell may be erased into a low threshold (high conduction) state by applying a positive potential to its gate which has the effect of attracting electrons from the substrate into the silicon dioxide/nitride interface and trapping a negative charge there. A trapped negative charge has the same effect as negative gate bias on a MOSFET and therefore aids the normal negative gate bias with the result that the transistor is held in a high conduction (on) state and has a switching threshold of approximately -2 V.

Therefore information is stored in an EAROM in a similar manner to that used in a EPROM, except that the trapped charges are induced by gate potentials rather than by avalanching. For this reason an EAROM may be selectively erased and reprogrammed since all gates are electrically accessible via a matrix decoding mechanism.

Problem 16 Sketch the construction of a typical 4 bit (2×2 matrix) magnetic core store.

The construction of a typical magnetic core store is shown in *Fig 18*.

Problem 17 Explain how digital information is stored in a magnetic core store and how **'coincident current selection'** is used as a means of addressing.

The basic storage element in a magnetic core store is a small torroid (or core) approximately 2 mm diameter, made from a magnetic material called **'ferrite'**.

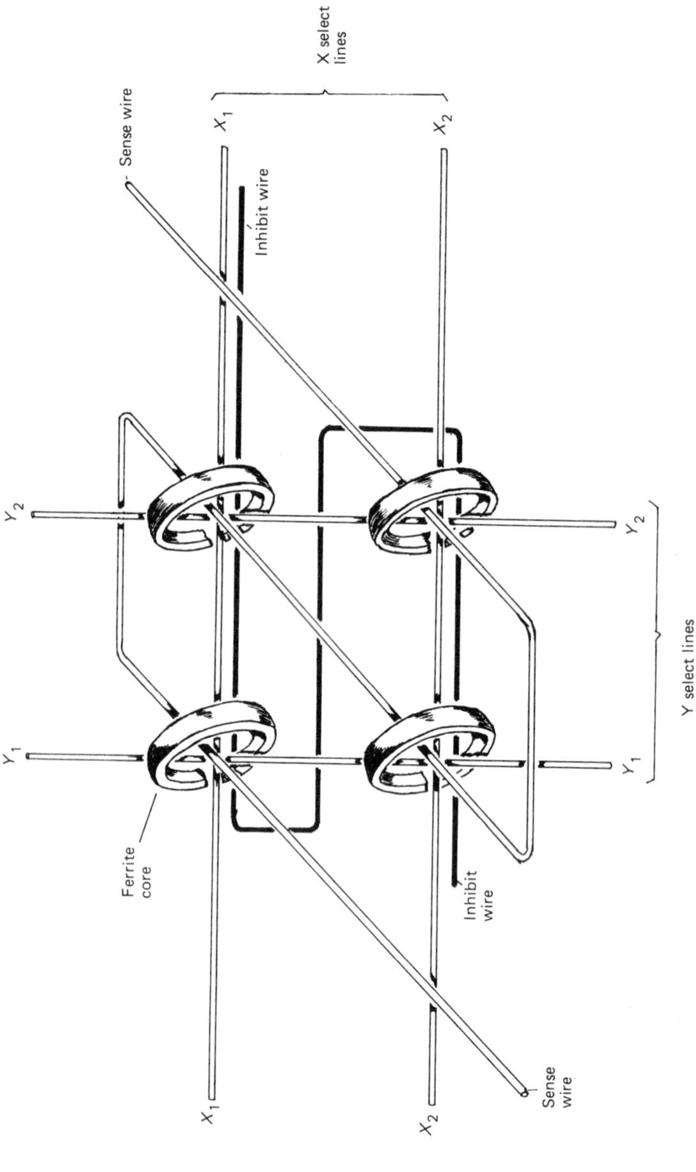

Fig 18

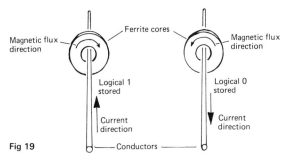

Fig 19

Information is stored in each core by magnetising it in one direction for a logical 0, and in the opposite direction for a logical 1. Magnetisation of a core is achieved by passing current along a conductor which passes through its centre (see *Fig 19*).

Since a very large number of cores are used in a typical store, a system of addressing is required so that information may be written into a single specified core. Addressing is achieved by arranging a core store in the form of a matrix of X and Y selection wires with one X and one Y selection wire passing through the centre of each core (see *Fig 20*).

The magnetic hysteresis (B/H) curve of an ideal ferrite core is shown in *Fig 21*, and it can be seen that a current change of I is required to change the stored data from a logical 1 to a logical 0 or vice versa (anything less than I causes only a temporary change).

To address a particular core, a current of $\tfrac{1}{2}I$ is passed along one X and one Y select wire. The core through which these two wires are threaded receives a

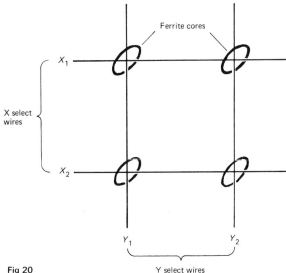

Fig 20

161

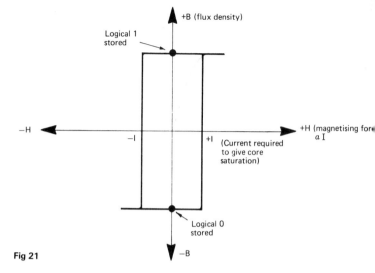

Fig 21

total through current of ($\frac{1}{2}I + \frac{1}{2}I$). All other cores in the store have a through current of $\frac{1}{2}I$ or 0, neither of which causes any change in their cores. Therefore only one core in the matrix receives sufficient current to cause a change in its stored logic level (see *Fig 22*).

This is a system known as **'coincident current selection'** since only the core in which the two selection currents coincide is able to receive new data.

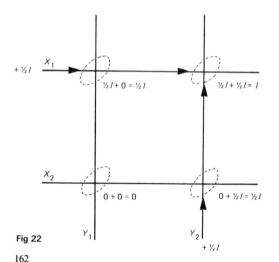

Fig 22

Problem 18 With reference to a magnetic core store, explain how the contents of a store may be read and why rewriting of data must be carried out after each read operation.

A location in a magnetic core store is read by writing a logical 0 into that location using coincident current addressing. If the core in that location was previously storing a logical 1, a reversal of the direction of the stored magnetic field occurs, otherwise no change takes place. A third wire, known as a **'sense wire'** or **'read wire'** is threaded through all of the cores in the store matrix, and an emf is induced in this wire if a change in direction of the magnetic flux occurs. Thus an emf is induced in the sense wire only if a logical 1 was previously stored, and is used to set a read flip flop (see *Fig 23*). The Q output of this flip flop is set if the store location contained a logical 1, but reset if the location contained a logical 0.

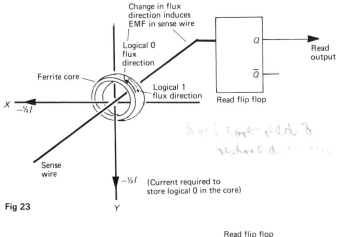

Fig 23

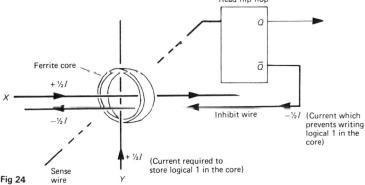

Fig 24

It can be seen that this method of reading a core causes it to be erased and it is therefore necessary to rewrite the lost information by following each read operation with a restore cycle. A restore cycle consists of writing a logical 1 back into each core once it has been read. If, however, the core previously stored a logical 0, the restore cycle must be prevented from storing a logical 1 in the core. Therefore a fourth wire, called an **'inhibit wire'** is threaded through all cores in the matrix, and is connected to the $\overline{Q}$ output of the read flip flop (see *Fig 24*).

Reading a core which has a logical 0 stored in it causes $\overline{Q}$ of the read flip flop to become logical 1 (since Q is logical 0), and this causes a current of $-\frac{1}{2}I$ to flow in the inhibit wire. This current of $-\frac{1}{2}I$ is in direct opposition to the $+\frac{1}{2}I$ current in the X select wire and this has the effect of preventing a logical 1 from being written into the core during the restore cycle. Reading a core which has a logical 1 stored in it causes Q to become logical 0 (since Q is logical 1) which prevents any current from flowing in the inhibit wire. Therefore a logical 1 is stored in the core which reinstates the information lost during the read cycle.

C FURTHER PROBLEMS ON DIGITAL STORAGE DEVICES

(a) SHORT ANSWER PROBLEMS

1 A digital storage device which loses its stored information if its power supply is interrupted is known as a . . . . . . memory.

2 The selection of one particular location in a digital storage system is generally called . . . . . .

3 ROM, PROM and EPROM are all examples of a . . . . . . memory.

4 The technique used by a manufacturer to store information in a ROM is known as . . . . . .

5 An EPROM may be erased by the use of . . . . . .

6 In order to retain the stored data in a dynamic RAM, a system of . . . . . . is required.

7 A random access memory (RAM) is more correctly called a . . . . . .

8 In order to reduce the number of connections to a digital storage system, a . . . . . . is normally used.

9 In a core store, information is stored in the form of . . . . .

10 After reading data out of a core store it is necessary to perform a . . . . . .

(b) CONVENTIONAL PROBLEMS

1 Explain the uses of the following types of digital storage devices:
(a) static RAM,
(b) dynamic RAM,
(c) ROM,
and (d) EPROM.

2. Using manufacturers data sheets, compare a bipolar RAM with a MOS RAM in terms of:
   (i) storage capacity,
   (ii) speed of access,
   and (iii) power consumption.

3. Compare the different techniques used to program the following devices:
   (a) ROM,
   (b) PROM,
   and (c) EPROM.

4. Explain the differences between:
   (a) volatile and non-volatile memories,
   and (b) static and dynamic memories.

Index

Accumulator, 137
Address, 143
Addressing, 142
AND-gate, 15
Assynchronous binary counter, 97, 107
    sequential logic circuit, 73
Avalanche injection programming, 154

Binary counters, 95
Bi-quinary counter, 114
Bistables, 73
Boolean algebra, laws of, 1

'Carry store' bistable, 137
CLEAR input, 90
Clocked R-S bistable, 73
CML, 41
CMOS, 39, 40, 58
    counter, 100
    decade counter, 123
    registers, 138
Coincident current selection, 159
Column select signal, 143
Combinational logic networks, 17
Counters, 95
Couple, 2

D-type bistable, 73, 74, 81
Decade counter, 100
De Morgan's laws, 14, 18
Digital stopwatch, 119
    storage devices, 140
'Down count', 97
Dynamic hazards, 107
    RAM, 140, 148

EAROM, 141, 158
ECL, 39, 41
Edge triggering, 88, 89
EPROM, 141, 155

FAMOS, 156
Fan out, 55
Ferrite, 159
    core store, 141
Field programmable, 141
Flip flop, 73
Full adder circuit, 137
Fusible link programming, 154

Inhibit wire, 164
Invert gate, 16

J-K bistable, 73, 74, 84
Johnson counter, 123, 135

Karnaugh maps, 1, 26, 76, 82, 86
    procedure, 5

Latch, 73
Logic circuits, 14
    families, 39

Magnetic core store, 159
Mask programming, 154
Master slave circuit, 75, 88, 91
Memory cells, 140, 143
Module, 110
MOSFET, 59

NAND-gate, 16, 23
Noise, 52
    margin, 52
Non-volatile memory circuit, 140
NOR-gate, 16, 27
NOT-gate, 16

OR-gate, 15
Oscillation, 87

PIPO register, 125
PISO register, 125
PRESET input, 90
Presettable counter, 117
PROM, 141, 154
Propagation delay, 107

RAM, 140, 142
'Read mostly' memory, 141
Read wire, 163
'Read-write' memory, 140, 143
Refreshing, 140, 149
Registers, 125
Reset, 73
Ring counter, 134
'Ripple-through' counter, 97
ROM, 140, 152
'Row select' signal, 143
R-S bistable, 73, 75

Schottky diode, 57
Sense wire, 163
Sequential logic, 73
Set, 73
Shift register, 125
SIPO register, 125
SISO register, 125
Static RAM, 140, 148
Switch debouncing, 91
Synchronous binary counter, 97, 107
Synchronous decade counter, 110
Synchronous sequential logic circuits, 73
System clock, 73

Threshold potential, 158
Totem pole output stage, 45, 46

Transitional counts, 107
TTL, 39, 43, 55
   counter, 100
   register, 132
T-type bistable, 74, 83
'Twisted ring' counter, 123, 135

Unit load, 55
Universal logic gates, 17
'Up count', 97

Volatile memory circuit, 140

'Weighted' counters, 97
Wired-OR output, 49